Satyam Sanatanam

Answers on Sanatana Dharma

Sri Mata Amritanandamayi Devi

Mata Amritanandamayi Center
San Ramon, California, United States

Satyam Sanatanam (The Eternal Truth)
Answers on Sanatana Dharma
Sri Mata Amritanandamayi Devi

Malayalam original: Satyam Sanatanam
(Second Edition)
Compiled by: Swami Jnanamritananda Puri
English translation by: Rajani Menon

Published by
Mata Amritanandamayi Center
P.O. Box 613
San Ramon, CA 94583-0613 USA

International: www.amma.org
In India: www.amritapuri.org

Contents

Foreword

The ancient seers of Bhārat gifted to the world the magnificent message:

> *ēkam sat viprā bahudhā vadanti*
>
> That which exists is one; sages call it by various names.

This message is now distant from the collective mind of society and of the individual, and is the fundamental reason for many of the contemporary problems linked to religion. Even when we say that modern scientific technology has transformed the world into a global village, human hearts are becoming increasingly distant from each other.

"Vasudhaiva kuṭumbakam – the world is one family" is the concept Bhārat has given to the world. This outlook is founded on the basis of the essential oneness of humanity and the union of human hearts. The ultimate solution for all of the world's problems is to accept and imbibe this awareness of oneness. If that is not possible, we should at least develop a mental attitude of tolerance towards diverse viewpoints and doctrines. The principles of Sanātana Dharma that were given to us through the enlightened words of our ancient seers will lead us in this direction. They are the beacons that light the path to human perfection. Sanātana Dharma proclaims the eternal truths that all can accept regardless of religion and caste, and that we all can practice in our lives.

This new edition of *Satyam Sanātanam* also contains answers to questions that devotees asked Amma in different situations after the first edition's publication. Heeding Amma's words, ashram residents give talks on various topics at the Amritapuri ashram. One of the main topics of 2021 was Sanātana Dharma. One evening, during a talk by a resident, Amma graciously spoke for a long time on the topic of Sanātana Dharma. A concise summary of her words is given under the heading 'The Greatness of Sanātana Dharma.' This serves as the introduction to this second edition.

Undoubtedly, we will get a clear view of Sanātana Dharma from this collection of Amma's words.

Swami Jnanamritananda Puri

The Greatness of Sanātana Dharma

Sri Mata Amritanandamayi Devi

The Hindu religion differs from other religions in that it is Sanātana Dharma, the eternal way that enlightens us with many life principles that are equally relevant to all human beings. Without understanding this truth, many consider Sanātana Dharma to be a religion. When other religions arrived here and built walls, the Hindu religion also seemed to be enclosed within a wall.

There used to be only one home on spacious land, and no fences were needed to create boundaries. A group of people came from far away. They built a house in front of that first home and started living there. They also built a fence around it and began calling themselves the people from the East House. After some time, another group arrived and built another house behind the original one. They also constructed a fence around their house, and called themselves people from the West House. Without much delay, even more settlers arrived and built houses to the north and south of the original home. They also fenced in their houses and became known as the North House people and South House people. The people who originally lived on the land did not build any fences. But regrettably, it was those who never built a fence that came to be known as the people within the fence. This is the current state of Sanātana Dharma. Even though Sanātana Dharma has not built any fences, it can now only be known as the "Hindu religion."

When the settlers arrived from all four directions and built their own houses and fences, those who had been living there originally were also enclosed within those fences and began to lose their own identity. They too needed to construct their own fences and pathways, for otherwise they would not be able to sustain their way of life. Amma feels that this kind of reasoning motivates those who believe in Sanātana Dharma to state their case in the same manner as the followers of other religions. Sanātana Dharma is, by nature, all-inclusive. It accepts and includes diverse viewpoints. Through the ages, people have traveled from this land to many other countries, but they have never destroyed the civilizations of those countries. They have never looted the wealth of those countries and taken it back with them.

Śhrī Rāma went to Laṅka, killed Rāvaṇa, and conquered the land, but he did not bring anything back from there. He crowned Rāvaṇa's brother, Vibhīṣhaṇa, as king. He flew with Sītā back to Ayōdhyā in the puṣhpaka-vimāna (the flying chariot of Rāvaṇa), but did not make it his own; he sent it back to Laṅka. This is the example Śhrī Rāma set for us. But those who invaded Bhārat looted all its wealth and took it away. They tried to turn this land into a desert. It may be because they had to endure such persecution that the people of this land also thought about the need to organize themselves like those of other religions.

Amma does not find any fault when people from other religions say that their religion is the best. It is their belief. But Amma cannot accept the fact that in order to establish that only their religion is good, they find fault with, mock and denounce other religions. It is equal to saying that my mother is good, but your mother is a prostitute. It will only incite hatred. Religions must help to augment goodness equally in both believers and others.

When religions try to breed dislike and hatred, they descend to the level of mere organizations that demonstrate their strength by putting on a show. If religions aim for the welfare of the human race, how can they denounce anyone? How can they brand anyone as a non-believer and use violence against them? When everyone is a child of God, a true believer should be able to respect even those who do not believe in their faith.

Every religion includes all kinds of people. We need not see this as a drawback of religion. Human beings have different characters. No human is identical with another. Diversity is intrinsic to human nature. For example, every religion has business people who believe in their faith. There are those who have incurred losses in their business, and those who have gained; there are healthy people and sick people; there are those who have love for others; and there are criminals.

Quarrels and conflicts arise when the people of one religion try to establish supremacy over another, saying theirs is the only true religion. Each individual is free to follow the faith he or she likes, and to practice the observances and prayers of that faith. However, such prayers and rituals should never create difficulties for others. It should never be that they are performed while mocking and denouncing others.

A human being should know who he or she is. Know yourself — then you will know that nothing is separate from you. This is true religion.

For those who follow Sanātana Dharma, dharma[1] itself is of the utmost importance. Sanātana Dharma does not have the narrow-mindedness of a religion. As God pervades the entire universe, followers of Sanātana Dharma try to see God in all living beings. They do not exclude any segment of society. They recognize that all is one — it is the one divine consciousness that resides in everyone. But others do not understand this.

The majority of those whose faith is Hinduism do not have the right knowledge of the Hindu religion. Therefore, those from other religions who wish to spread their own faith, try to exploit them. Unlike other religions, the Hindu religion is not an organized religion. Those who believe

---

[1] 'That which upholds (creation)' — dharma generally refers to the harmony of the universe, a righteous code of conduct, sacred duty, or the eternal law.

in Hinduism do not have to live according to the advice given by their religious leaders.

Children of other religions learn about their religion from a very early age. Classes teaching the fundamentals of their religion are methodically organized. The religious priests can question those who do not attend those classes. Those religions give their priests the authority to do so. Whereas Hindu families have only scanty knowledge of their traditional rituals and observances, whatever has been passed down in families from one generation to the next. Often, it will not be proper knowledge. Children learn from their parents and their children learn from them. But no one enlightens them on the spiritual principles behind these traditional rituals and observances. They do not know those principles.

Long ago, when the gurukula[2] system of education existed, the values of Sanātana Dharma were imparted along with regular education. But there is no avenue for this in modern times. This is why people from other religions find it easy to find fault with those traditions and rituals,

[2] Traditional school where children live with a guru who instructs them in scriptural and academic knowledge, while instilling spiritual values.

and convince Hindus that they are wrong. They exploit the Hindus' lack of knowledge about the Hindu religion and convert them to the belief that their religion alone is true.

Diseases attack and overcome a weak body. Germs fear a healthy body with excellent immunity. No disease can conquer a fit body. So, we must eat good food and exercise properly to increase our health. Likewise, if others are exploiting our ignorance of our own religion, the remedy is to learn what our own religion is and to teach others. It is to know the spiritual principles behind the traditional rituals and observances.

Sanātana Dharma is older than every other religion in the world now. Its existence for tens of thousands of years and continuing existence today reveals the greatness of the Hindu religion. It is a crime to be born into such a great religion and remain ignorant of its glory.

Amma's path is the middle path. For Amma, everyone is her child. She accepts and embraces everyone and does not coerce anyone. Amma does not tell anyone that "this is needed and that is not." Amma will never say that one should convert others. It is possible to love everyone and everything without conversion. This is the feeling, the mental attitude that we should awaken. This is true religion. However, everyone should know the mother who gave birth to them. They should know their birth mother's address. Where have I come from? Where is my mother's maternal home? Where is my mother now? We should be able to answer these questions to anyone. We are indebted to do so. Otherwise, we will be like those born without a father or mother. Once we know ourselves, we will know that no one is separate from us. Knowing this is true religion. The ignorance of this truth is the reason for all conflict, inter-religious and also within the same religion.

Amma travels to many foreign countries. When I go to Spain and some other places, people come to me and say, "Amma, our religions are lost. Our ancestor's religion does not exist anymore." They showed me the idols of the deities their ancestors worshiped. It is indeed amazing that with God's grace, eighty percent of the people of Bhārat held on to their faith. People from foreign lands have repeatedly invaded Bhārat. They ruled Bhārat for centuries. They killed millions of people. Even then, the people of this land endured and held on. The people who lived in those times had such overwhelming love, faith, and surrender to their saṁskāra (culture) and to their traditional lineage of gurus.

Ordinary humanity has lost faith in the traditions and lineages of gurus. Maybe this is the reason for Sanātana Dharma's current state. The people do not understand the benefit of the guru paramparā (traditional lineage of teachers of spiritual wisdom), and those who know do not try to make others understand. Nowadays, many stand within the fencing of caste and clan. Even now, some sannyāsīs[3] harbor such thoughts of caste. Those from a higher caste do not come and work among the lower strata of society. This notion of caste is the curse of the Hindu religion. The sannyāsīs of today should prepare themselves to see all those who believe in the Hindu faith as equals and work amongst them without the prejudices of caste and clan. They should be willing to bring the values of Sanātana Dharma into their midst.

---

[3] A monk who has taken formal vows of renunciation. A sannyāsī traditionally wears an ochre-colored cloth representing the "fire of renunciation" — the burning away of all attachments.

From her childhood onwards, Amma used to go to the nearby homes, sweep the area clean, then gather up and bring back the dry leaves and other litter to her home. Amma would make a fire pit near the south side of the Kaḷari[4] of Amma's home and burn it all, like an eternal flame. This was Amma's sacrificial fire. Amma would go to sixty houses nearby to collect tapioca leaves and kāḍi veḷḷam (raw rice water) to feed the cows. When Amma saw the misery and hardship in those homes, Amma started bringing things from her own home to give to them. Amma also got some beatings at home for this reason. In those days, a question for nature arose from Amma's mind: Why were these people suffering? If everything was God's creation, why did only a few suffer?

During this time I disliked myself. I was in a state where I did not want to see anyone. Then the answer came from within: "It is their

---

[4] Formerly a cowshed belonging to Amma's birth house, it became a small temple where Amma started giving bhāva darśhan, embracing her devotees while revealing her oneness with Kṛiṣhṇa and Dēvī. It is also the place in the Amritapuri āśhram where daily fire rituals are conducted to date.

karma-phala, the fruit of their own actions." I immediately asked a counter question: "Someone runs carelessly and falls down. Is it our dharma to be mere onlookers, saying that falling down is their karma-phala?" The answer came immediately from within: "Your dharma, your responsibility is to lift up the fallen person." This was not just some crazy thought I had; it was a clear and direct answer to my question.

Up until this moment, Amma was disgusted even with Nature. Amma would spit on the earth, burrow a hole in the ground and try to sit inside it. Amma does not have the strength to see people suffering. Amma suffered terrible agony from their pain, the pain of poor people, people who could not get treated for diseases because they had no money. So many people were undergoing pain. Those who should have lived till eighty died at forty because they became sick. Amma saw many such instances. This is why Amma became the way she is today.

When a person has fallen to the ground, there is no need to see if it is a man or a woman as we lift them up from the ground. Our dharma in this instance is to save the fallen person. This is our responsibility. Sanātana Dharma aims to uplift each person to feel this sense of responsibility towards others. In Sanātana Dharma, there are no fences separating humankind in the name of religion. But when others built fences, it became impossible to survive without a fence. This may be the reason why frameworks were designed for Sanātana Dharma also. Instead of loving and serving not only humanity, but all beings in creation, religions have become akin to corporate companies. Their only aim is their own growth and survival. If others suffer due to their growth, they turn a blind eye to it. To gain more is their only aim.

Hindus honor all religious beliefs. They respect temples, churches, and mosques. They do not hesitate to respect everything and do not feel any hatred. This is because in Sanātana Dharma, creation and creator are not two, but one. In this universe, there is nothing separate from God. Sanātana Dharma teaches us that God resides in stones, blades of grass, trees, humanity, and all living beings. Therefore, we cannot see anything as separate. This is a culture that has come down through the generations. It is needed for the continued existence of this universe. Sanātana Dharma aims for a state in which nothing can be seen as other than ourselves. Nothing is separate from us. It is a state in which the individual "I" no longer exists; it is a state in which everything is contained within us. In such a state, there is nothing separate from us. Through our human birth, we should strive to attain this state of non-duality. This can be possible only if we let go of the duality of "I" and "You." Nothing but God exists here. If we reject anyone, we are denouncing God.

Even though many foreign powers ruled Bhārat, unlike in other countries, they were unable to annihilate our culture entirely. The kings and the people of this land resisted the foreign powers, due to the strong saṁskāra (character refinement) that was prevalent in their families.

There are four āśhrama dharmas (dharmas pertaining to four distinct stages of life) in Sanātana Dharma. They are brahmacharya – the life of the celibate student; gārhasthya – the life of a householder; vānaprastha – life in a forest or withdrawal from worldly responsibilities; and sannyāsa – the life of an ascetic. After brahmacharya, they enter gṛihasthāśhrama (the stage of life dedicated to being a gṛihastha – a householder). Once the children are born, they are brought up well, and both worldly education and spiritual knowledge are imparted to them. Once the children have entered married life, the parents enter the stage of vānaprastha. Finally, they accept sannyāsa. This is how they end their lives. Nowadays, even when parents become old, their bond is to their children, not to God. Neither do they imbibe spirituality, nor do they impart it to their children. This is the reason for their sorrow.

Children are no longer an assistance to their aged parents. When their aged parents become an inconvenience, children send them to old-age homes. This was not the case when joint families existed. There were people in the house to take care of the elders. Times have changed. We have lost our values and spiritual thoughts. It is this lack that we see reflected in society now.

But there is no need for my children to keep thinking about it and feel depressed. As much as possible, each of you should imbibe the principles of Sanātana Dharma and its values. Impart these values and principles to the coming generations. This will lead us to peace. If so, Sanātana Dharma will shine brighter than before. A culture exists and survives through people who live according to its ideals. Do not forget this. Children, the survival and continuation of Sanātana Dharma is through each one of you. Each one of my children should strive for this. This is all that Amma has to say.

Answers on Sanātana Dharma

1

Question: What is the difference between the Hindu religion and other religions?

Amma: The teachings that mahātmās gave to their disciples and followers later developed into different religions. In Bhārat, the eternal principles revealed to many mahātmās through their own experience came to be known as "Sanātana Dharma." Sanātana means eternal, that which lasts forever. It came to be known as the Hindu religion when other religions arrived in India, that's all. In reality, it is not a religion like the others. It is more appropriate to call it Hindu dharma rather than Hindu religion.

Because of this, the Hindu religion is not known in the name of a prophet or the founder of a religion. The foundation of the Hindu religion are the doctrines of the many seers who lived in Bhārat. Most religions have one foundational text. The foundational text of the Hindu religion can be said to be the *Vēdas*. However, the *Vēdas* were difficult for ordinary humans to understand. So later on, many more books were written for the benefit of common people. This is how the *Purāṇas* and *Itihāsas* gained popularity. Thus, the *Bhagavad Gītā*, embedded in the *Mahābhārata* (one of the two Itihāsas, the other being the *Rāmāyaṇa*), became an authoritative text accepted by all Hindus. The Hindu religion is constantly replenished by the teachings of the many mahātmās who have lived in different centuries. In this manner, the Hindu religion has acquired the tremendous wealth of countless spiritual texts of great merit.

Many religions believe that God is seated in heaven. In the Hindu religion however, God is pure consciousness transcending time and space; God is without attributes and without form; He[1] is all-pervading and omnipresent; God is the indweller in all living beings.

Most religions believe that those who live according to the principles of their religion and perform meritorious deeds will attain heaven after death. They can live there forever after,

---

[1] Amma has said that God is beyond any definition of gender. However, when Amma talks, she refers to God in the more traditional way, using the word 'He.'

enjoying various pleasures. But if they perform sinful actions, then they go to eternal hell after death. Religions like Hinduism and Buddhism believe in the law of karma. According to the law of karma, the cause for the joy and sorrow experienced by each person are the actions performed by them. Good actions bring joy, and wicked actions result in sorrow. One experiences joy and comfort due to the meritorious deeds performed in this life or previous lives. One experiences sorrow as a result of bad deeds. When we look at it this way, our own actions are the fundamental cause of our joys and sorrows.

From the perspective of the Hindu religion, each jīva (individual soul) takes birth again and again, depending on its previous actions. Just as someone discards an old set of clothes and puts on a new set, the jīva abandons its present body and accepts a new one — the jīva is reborn. According to the merits and demerits of actions performed by the jīva, it is reborn as a human, a bird, or an animal.

The Hindu religion does not consider anyone a sinner. This is because, fundamentally, each jīva is of the nature of God. It is eternally pure and free. But usually, humans are deluded to believe themselves to be the physical body and succumb to the fear of death. This ignorance of their true nature is the reason why jīvas take birth in different bodies and experience joy and sorrow. When this ignorance is destroyed, the jīva merges with God; the jīva transcends good and evil and becomes eternally free. This is known as God-realization or self-realization. Sanātana Dharma says that this is the highest goal of human life.

In Hindu religion, God does not have any particular name or form. But the all-powerful one can take on any form. Therefore, Hindu religion gives the freedom to worship God in any name and form. The Hindu religion is like a supermarket. You can get everything there.

Another unique feature of the Hindu religion is that there are many ways to gain God- or self-realization. Some religions emphasize prayer, while others focus on physical acts of worship, such as prostration in prayer. There are strict directives on which days they should go to their places of worship. But the Hindu religion does not have any such stipulations. Those who want to worship God can do so. It can be through prayer, prostration, sacred chants, or devotional singing.

It can be through systematic ritualistic worship or through mental worship. There are many ways of worship.

God can be worshiped as the one without qualities, or possessing qualities. We can visualize God with form and worship him. We can adore God as Śhiva, Viṣhṇu, Dēvī, Gaṇēśha, or any form we like. We can worship God in the temple, or we can worship God at home. We can worship him as formless, or with form. Instead of worshiping God, we can also follow the path of self-inquiry. There is no coercion to believe in God. You can meditate, or follow the path of selfless service. In this manner, the Hindu religion allows each individual to uplift themself from their present state by following any path they like. Likewise, unlike in other religions, to become a Hindu, there are no formal rituals.

2

Question: Who is the founder of the Hindu religion?

Amma: Unlike other religions, the Hindu religion was not formed in the name of a prophet or a mahātmā. Most world religions have a founder, and the foundations of that religion will be their teachings. However, the Hindu religion does not have any particular founder or prophet. Sanātana Dharma brings together the spiritual truths that the ancient ṛiṣhis of Bhārat realized through direct experiences. It also contains their teachings. Much later, it came to be called the Hindu religion. Those who followed Sanātana Dharma came to be known as Hindus.

Even though the principles of Sanātana Dharma were received from many ṛiṣhis, each one experienced the same fundamental truth. They saw that there was a changeless substratum to this constantly changing universe. They named it brahman.

The refrigerator cools objects, the heater heats, the light illumines, and the fan blows a breeze. However, the same electric current makes them all function. Even though their motors and functions are different and they have different prices, the same current flows through them. To know this, we must understand the attributes of electricity. Likewise, even though every object in this world may seem different to the eyes, the inner consciousness that dwells within each and every one of them is the same. This vision based on knowledge, called jñānadṛiṣhṭi, can be gained only through sādhanā, which is an intense, disciplined, and focused spiritual practice.

The great ṛiṣhis who experienced this truth, passed it down through the generations. The way of life of the ordinary people of the land of Bhārat was formulated based on this vision of oneness experienced by the great sages. Those who follow this saṁskāra (culture) based on the underlying oneness of all beings are known as Hindus. To put it briefly, the Hindu religion is not founded in the name of any religious figure or founder, or based on any single religious text. The Hindu dharma is the sum total of the sanātana (eternal) values of life.

3

Question: Is Sanātana Dharma the same as the Hindu religion?

Amma: Yes, the Hindu religion is Sanātana Dharma. It was only much later that it came to be called the Hindu religion. It is suitable for all places and all times. Sanātana Dharma teaches eternal truths that are capable of uplifting all of humanity. Sanātana Dharma aims for the welfare and advancement of all living beings, including humankind. It is not intolerant and narrow-minded, and it does not engage in sectarianism.

The mantras gifted by the ancient sages to the world are:

ōm asatōmā sadgamaya
tamasōmā jyōtirgamaya
mṛityōrmā amṛitaṁ gamaya

Lead us from untruth to truth,
Lead us from darkness to light,
Lead us from death to immortality.

ōm lōkāḥ samastāḥ sukhinō bhavantu

May all beings in all the worlds be happy.

ōm pūrṇamadaḥ pūrṇamidaṁ
pūrṇātpūrṇamudacyatē
pūrṇasya pūrṇamādāya
pūrṇamēvāvaśhiṣhyatē

That is the whole, this is the whole,
From the whole the whole has arisen,
Take away the whole from the whole,
And the whole alone remains.

From their words, we can see that they could not see anyone or any being as separate; there is not even a glimpse of differentiation. This darśhana, this spiritual vision, grew and thrived in Bhārat. When other religions entered this land, to distinguish Sanātana Dharma from them, it came to be called the Hindu religion.

Sanātana Dharma is simultaneously the world's most ancient and also an ever-new religion. Its goal is the welfare and prosperity of the entire world. Sanātana Dharma presents before the world a vision of unity, a vision of oneness, where every living being is linked to each other. It proclaims that all that we see is the one divine consciousness. Compassion towards all living beings arose from this vision of equality. All of creation are but different facets of the same truth — therefore, our culture taught us to honor and worship even the smallest creature. When the left hand is hurting, the right hand reaches out to caress it because both are parts of the same body. Likewise, the joy and sorrow of one are the joy and sorrow of the other. Sanātana Dharma teaches us to see the pain of others as our own pain, and the joy of others as our own joy, and to love and serve everyone.

4

Question: Aren't the different paths in Hinduism a drawback?

Amma: Never. It shows the Hindu religion's comprehensive nature and expansive, all-inclusive vision. This broad vision has sustained the foundational precepts and principles of the Hindu religion without any distortion or attenuation, even though it is thousands of years old. As time evolves, necessary changes will happen, but the foundational knowledge and principles are changeless. Customs and the performance of religious rituals may change according to time and place. It is the one divine consciousness that resides in all — this supreme knowledge is never lost.

Sanātana Dharma is firmly established in this changeless, eternal truth. At the same time, it is a saṁskāra, a culture that willingly accepts change and is ready to reform and renew itself. Sanātana Dharma is unique in its expansive vision and the logical reasoning of its scriptural texts.

Sanātana Dharma aims to uplift people from the planes of their current culture and mental maturity. Therefore, it contains concepts, ideals, and rituals suitable for every stratum of society. When we think logically, we realize the practical benefit behind each of them. This is how many paths and kinds of spiritual practices came into being.

When values diminish in society, mahātmās take birth to show the right way. The river keeps flowing, but its water is polluted by waste thrown from its banks. If we remove these contaminants, the water will regain its purity. This is the action performed by the mahātmās who have lived in the past and those who are living today. They clean the impurities from humanity's mind. When the mind becomes pure, a person will know God — because there is nothing other than God in this universe. There are many different ways by which this purification process happens. It will be a different path for each human being. The goal of the Hindu religion is to lead humanity to realize its true nature, God. This is the way to supreme peace.

5

Question: Why does the Hindu religion have many paths?

Amma: The goal of the Hindu religion is the ultimate release from suffering of each jīva – atyantikā duḥkha nirvṛtti – the complete cessation of sorrow. This can be gained even when we are alive. In Sanātana Dharma, it is called mōkṣha (liberation). Sanātana Dharma does not insist that there is only one way to mōkṣha. The guru advises a path best suited to each individual based on their physical condition, their mental maturity, and their intellectual level. It is not possible to open every lock with a single key. Likewise, to open our hearts, we need a path suitable to our level of knowledge and suitable to our culture.

A river with only one course does not benefit many people. But if it branches out into many smaller channels, it will benefit all the people living on its banks. Likewise, because the gurus advise different paths, the teachings are understood and assimilated by many more people. We need to teach a deaf child through sign language, and a blind child can be taught only through braille. If it is a mentally challenged child, we need to go down to its level and teach in very simple and patient ways. Only then will the child understand what it is being taught. Likewise, the gurus decide upon the course best suited for someone by considering their abilities, mental attitudes, and culture. The paths may differ, but the goal remains the same — the supreme truth is one.

Clothes tailored to the same measure will not fit everyone. As one grows, the clothes one wears need to change. Likewise, paths and spiritual observances will have to be modified according to the times. This is the contribution that mahātmās make to Sanātana Dharma. This breadth of vision is the hallmark of Hindu Dharma. If we feed meat to a breastfeeding infant, it will not be able to digest it. It will fall sick and will also become a matter of concern and hardship for others. Therefore, many kinds of food are needed, based on our ability to digest and according to differences in tastes and preferences. Only then can everyone maintain their health. Likewise in Sanātana Dharma, the traditions of worship are varied as they are based on each one's innate culture. Each one can accept what suits them. Every type of character can receive the religious observances most suited to them from Sanātana Dharma. This is how jñāna yōga, karma yōga, bhakti yōga, rājā yōga, haṭha yōga, kuṇḍalinī yōga, kriyā yōga, svara yōga, mantra, tantra, and many other spiritual paths came into being in Sanātana Dharma.

Each person can adopt the practice or path most suited to them. They can also move forward by integrating many paths. Whatever the path, the goal is to stop the identification of oneself as the physical body, and to rise to the awareness of the self, or in other words, to attain God-realization.

6

Question: What is the unique feature of the Hindu religion?

Amma: The Hindu religion perceives divinity in all beings, both sentient and insentient, and sees them as God's manifestations. It teaches that this divinity is immanent in each human being and that anyone can realize it through self-effort. This unique feature, the perception of divinity in all beings, is the most essential aspect of Hinduism, setting it apart from other religions.

The Hindu religion does not see creation and creator as two separate entities. It is the creator who has become his creation. Fundamentally, all is one. This is called brahman, absolute reality. According to Hindu religion, knowing this non-dual truth (advaita satya) is the highest goal of human life. Gold is inherent in all golden ornaments. A gold ornament is never separate from the gold with which it is made. Likewise, there is nothing separate from God in this world. God is the one truth. The dream is not separate from the dreamer. But one should wake up to realize that one was dreaming. Because we have not awakened to this awareness, we see all that diversity surrounding us. We like some people and feel aversion towards others. Because of these likes and dislikes, joy and sorrow become the nature of our lives. But, when we awaken to our true essence, there is no longer you and me. All is God. Only bliss exists. To awaken to this experiential knowledge, the Hindu religion advises many paths suited for each person's saṁskāra – their mental and emotional state, and the circumstances of their life and upbringing. No other religion has such diversity in paths, religious traditions, and observances.

The supreme truth shines as the diverse universe. When the one sun is reflected in a thousand pots, there will be a thousand reflections. But in fact, there is only one sun. Likewise, it is the same supreme truth that illumines all objects. The Hindu religion calls this supreme truth brahman.

We can mold the figures of a donkey, a horse, a rat, a lion, etc., from clay. They are different in name and form, but they are all made of clay. We should have the vision to see the clay within all these diverse names and forms. Likewise, we should be able to transform the vision that sees this world of diverse forms and names differently and realize that the one divine consciousness has manifested as all this diversity.

In the Hindu religion, God is everything. There is nothing other than God. The Hindu dharma teaches us to see animals, birds, creatures that crawl, trees, plants, mountains, rivers... everything, even the deadly cobra, as God, and it teaches us to love and serve them.

Like the various parts of our body are not separate from us, when we gain the experience of supreme oneness, we will recognize that this universe is not separate from us. The awareness that had remained limited to our own body transcends all boundaries. It becomes all-inclusive, rejecting nothing. The mother experiences the child's pain as her own. Likewise, the mahātmās who have gained the realization of oneness with the universe, see the joy and sorrow of others as their own joy and sorrow. Compassion becomes their nature, inseparable from them as heat is to fire, cold is to water, and sweetness is to honey.

When our own finger pokes our eye, we will forgive the finger and caress our eye. Neither the eye nor the finger are separate from us. Similarly, the Hindu religion aims to elevate each individual to the state of seeing everyone as oneself. Human beings attain perfection when they elevate themselves from the confining thought that they are limited to this human body, and gain the experiential, blissful awareness of their oneness with God. Thus, the Hindu religion reveals the way for us to see God in the entire universe and gain the experience that we are not different but one with God. It shows us diverse paths to reach this oneness, be it karma yōga, the path of action; bhakti yōga, the path of devotion; jñāna yōga, the path of knowledge; or rāja yōga, the path of meditation.

The hallmark of Sanātana Dharma is unity in diversity. There are many languages, many traditions, and many ways of worship. Yet even in the midst of all this diversity, like the sweetness that binds together all the ingredients of the pañchāmṛitam[2], Sanātana Dharma unites our hearts. This is known as ārṣhasaṁskāra — the culture of refinement passed down to us by the great sages.

7

Question: What is the difference between brahman and īśhvara?

Amma: Brahman is the eternal substratum, the foundation of this universe. It is without form or qualities (nirguṇa) and does not act (niśhkriyā). Īśhvara, or God, is the same ultimate reality with form and qualities (saguṇa) and performs actions (sakriyā). Īśhvara is the creator, sustainer, and destroyer of this universe.

8

Question: What are the four goals of human life?

Amma: Most humans desire wealth and position. Likewise, everyone desires happiness in life.

---

[2] A mixture of five foods — milk, yogurt, honey, ghee, and sugar — that is offered during worship rituals and often distributed as prasād (blessed food).

Money and position constitute artha; happiness and creature comforts are kāma. There is nothing wrong in desiring or striving for artha and kāma, but Sanātana Dharma says clearly and firmly that artha and kāma should be gained and enjoyed only by following dharma. It also states that the highest goal of a human being is not gaining artha or kāma; the highest goal is to become one with God and to experience the bliss of the true self. This supreme goal is known as mōkṣha. In short, according to the Hindu religion, dharma, artha, kāma, and mōkṣha are the four objects to be pursued and realized in a human life. First and foremost, we should live by dharma. The supreme goal to be reached by a human life is mōkṣha. This is why dharma, artha, kāma, and mōkṣha are known as the four puruṣhārthas, the fourfold objects of human pursuit.

9

Question: What is dharma?

Amma: Dharma is that which sustains this world and all its beings. Dharma is the reason for the harmony among all living beings.

If all the vehicles on the road obey the traffic rules, there will be no traffic accidents, and every vehicle can drive safely. Likewise, if each human lives according to dharma instead of going after selfish goals, the world and the societies in which we live will maintain harmony. If all the parts of the body act according to their intrinsic dharma, the body will maintain its health. Likewise, if each member obeys their dharma, society as a whole will become a healthy organism; none will have to suffer unjustly.

Each living being has its own dharma. All beings except humans live according to their intrinsic nature. Only humans have been given the power of discernment. Therefore, human beings are duty-bound to act in a dharmic manner. The dharma of a lamp is to shed light; the dharma of our eyes is to see. The dharma of the heart is to pump blood so that it circulates throughout the entire body. We will be able to lead a healthy life only if each organ in our body performs its dharma properly. Likewise, the harmony of this universe can be maintained only if all the beings in this world fulfill their dharma correctly. The principle that is the cause of the harmony of this world was called dharma by the ancient seers of Bhārat.

Only if vehicles obey the traffic rules can they travel safely. Likewise, society can sustain itself and progress only if each individual member performs their dharma adequately. The nation will move forward on the path of progress only if each citizen lives a life established in dharma. It is the same for the family also. The family will only attain peace and prosperity if each member lives with the right values and empathy.

The teacher must fulfill his dharma as a teacher when he is in school. But his dharma will be different when he reaches home. To his children, he must fulfill his dharma as a father; to his siblings, he must fulfill his dharma as a brother. Thus, depending on the place and circumstances, his dharma differs. Dharma is the right action performed at the right time in the right manner. But there is one dharma that is paramount to every other. This is the paramadharma. It is the realization of the perfection, the blissful self within us. Suppose a butterfly lays an egg on a plant leaf. If it is destroyed in the egg stage itself, its life will not have been successful. If it dies in the worm or pupae stage, its life will not have been successful. When it emerges as a butterfly and displays the beauty of all the wonderful colors and capabilities latent within it, it attains the ultimate goal of its life. Its life has become successful.

Each one of us has divinity within. It is our true nature. The paramadharma, the supreme goal of each human being, is to realize their true nature. Pūrnatā (wholeness or perfection) does not mean our own liberation; it means the state in which we see everyone as our own self. But now, we are unable to see the real value of the wealth that is our life. We fritter our lives away in small pleasures.

Dharma is that which maintains the harmony and stability of the universe. Each individual desires joy and comfort and strives to gain them. However, when we gain them, we should not forget that others are entitled to the same joy and comfort, just like us. We are duty-bound to give back in the same measure that which we have accepted from society. If we are not willing to do so, the harmony of society will be in peril. However, if we give more than we take, peace and unity will prevail, and dharma will prosper.

10

Question: What is mōkṣha?

Amma: Eternal bliss is known as mōkṣha. It is our real nature, our svarūpa. When people say "I," they mean the body. But the body, mind, and intellect have been subject to many changes and continue to change. The "I" now differs from the "I" of ten years ago. The body has grown. The mental attitudes have shifted. Yet, even amid all this change, the true "I" does not change. The form of the unchanging pure consciousness, the substratum of all, is known as the ātman. Even when the body is destroyed, my real nature, the ātman, is indestructible.

The ātman is of the form of knowledge and of the form of bliss. There is not even a trace of sorrow in the ātman. But most humans are deluded into the belief that they are this body. This identification with the body is called ignorance or ajñāna. If ajñāna is removed, then we will be able to experience the blissful self. This ātmānanda (bliss of the self) has many names: mōkṣha, God-realization, self-realization, mukti. We can rise to that supreme state when we are alive. Such people who are liberated even while they are alive are known as jīvanmuktas. As long as the tadpole has a tail, it can only live in water. Once the tail is gone, the frog can live both on land and in water. Likewise, if we lose the tail of our ego, we are in bliss, whether we reside within the body or leave the body. A rubber ball will stay afloat in water, and remains intact when it falls to the ground. Likewise, nothing in this world can obstruct a jīvanmukta's ātmānanda, their inner bliss. Their bliss resides within them, not in the external objects of the world. This does not mean that they will not have body aches and pains, or that they will not have joy and sorrow. Joy and sorrow will come along when we take up a body. It is the nature of life. Yet, a jīvanmukta constantly experiences the inherently blissful self, regardless of the circumstances. This state is mōkṣha.

The scriptural texts state that the highest goal of human life is mōkṣha. The highest goal is not the attainment of heavenly pleasures after death or reaching the realm of your iṣhṭa-dēvatā (beloved deity). Mōkṣha is supreme bliss. It is the release from all types of bondage and sorrow.

Life is full of opposites. We cannot envision a world without joy and sorrow, life and death, day and night. If we realize that joy and sorrow are the nature of life, then we will be able to accept both with an even-minded outlook. We should understand spirituality and strive with awareness in order to reach this state. Spirituality is knowledge for the mind that needs to be imbibed. It is the science that teaches us to experience joy and contentment without being distraught by the ups and downs of life. It is the foremost thing we need to know in our life.

11

Question: The Hindu religion worships many Gods. In reality, is there more than one God?

Amma: The Hindu religion doesn't have many Gods. The Hindu religion believes in the One God. It proclaims that there is nothing other than God in this universe; it is God who has manifested as the entire universe. God is the omnipresent pure consciousness. He is above name and form. However, in order to bless his devotee, he can take up any form. He can take up as many forms as needed. He can accept as many bhāvas, as many divine moods and emotions, as he wants to. The wind can arrive as a gentle breeze, blow as a strong wind, or create havoc as a hurricane. The omnipotent God, who controls the wind, can manifest whatever bhāva he wants to. Who can describe his glory? God can be formless and with form, like the air that can remain still or blow as wind. Like water that can become ice or vapor. Thus, the one omnipotent God is worshiped in many forms and in many bhāvas, such as Śhiva, Viṣhṇu, Gaṇēśha, Muruga, Durgā, Sarasvatī, Kālī, etc.

Likes and dislikes vary from person to person, depending on the circumstances in which they grew up, their predilections, and the culture they acquired. This is why the Hindu religion gives everyone the freedom to worship God in any form and in any bhāva, in accordance with their preferences and mental maturity. This is how many īśhvara-bhāvas evolved in the Hindu religion. They are not different Gods. They are paths by which everyone can be uplifted from where they stand. A woman is a mother in her home, she is a wife, a sister, and a daughter. Her job role may be that of a teacher. The same woman stands in front of different people with different bhāvas, with different attitudes and mental inclinations. Likewise, the same īśhvara is worshiped in different bhāvas, with different names and different forms, confirming the devotee's mental image and heartfelt desire. That is all there is to it.

Īśhvara is the reason for the creation, sustenance, and destruction of the universe – on this fact, there will be no difference in opinion among those who believe in God. But doubts and differences of opinion arise regarding the svarūpa (essential nature) of īśhvara. What are his name, form, and qualities etc.?

In the Hindu religion, i.e. Sanātana Dharma, there is only one īśhvara. It does not have many Gods. Not only that, the Hindu religion teaches us that the one īśhvara manifests and shines as this world and all the occupants of this world – sentient and insentient. It teaches us that there is nothing separate from īśhvara in this universe.

Why do we find it difficult to see unity in diversity? Mud became the mountain, the mud house, the mud pot, and the clay idol. Similarly, the same īśhvara shines as the diverse forms of this universe.

In the Hindu religion, īśhvara has no particular name or form. He can be worshiped through any name and any form because God is the indivisible divine consciousness without name or form.

In reality, God cannot be comprehended by the mind or described in words. However, through the right spiritual practice, we will be able to realize God through an indescribable inner experience that is beyond words. Will a child be able to describe the extent of his pain or joy? Is it possible to describe in words the beauty of nature or the taste of honey? When we experience God, we recognize that our essential nature is one with the essential nature of God.

Even though God is beyond name and form, he will take on any form to bless his devotee. He will also take on any bhāva. An actor plays many roles, but he remains the same. Likewise, the same God is worshiped in many bhāvas and in many forms, such as Śhiva, Viṣhṇu, Dēvī, Śhrī Rāma, Śhrī Kṛiṣhṇa, etc.

We can easily visualize and worship God with form and qualities (saguṇa). A thirsty man will need a pot or will cup his hands to collect water from the river to quench his thirst. Likewise, through the means of a God with form, we can worship the One God and realize him.

In the same household, the father may like Śhiva, while the mother likes Kṛiṣhṇa. The elder son may like Dēvī, while the younger one likes Muruga. This is no problem if they realize that even though the forms and bhāvas are different, the underlying śhakti, or primal energy, is the same. There is no need to fear that if one worships Śhiva, Viṣhṇu will get angry, or that if one worships Kṛiṣhṇa, Gaṇēśha may not like it. We should have the firm conviction that, ultimately, they are all one.

It is good to accept one of the many forms of God as your cherished personal deity, your iṣhṭa-dēvatā. It can be any form, be it Śhiva, Viṣhṇu, Dēvī, Rāma, or any other. We should have the firm conviction that our iṣhṭa-dēvatā is īśhvara, God. In order to progress on the path of devotion, it is ideal to worship our iṣhṭa-dēvatā with love and discipline. This will make the mind one-pointed and firm. We will gain all that we need for our growth from our iṣhṭa-dēvatā.

A bird that went in search of prey damaged its wing in an unfortunate mishap. It was unable to fly. The sun was setting. The bird was upset because its nest was on the other side of the river and it couldn't fly across. The nestlings would be worried by not being able to see her, which increased the bird's anxiety. At this point, she saw an ice floe floating down the river. The bird somehow hopped onto the ice floe. A favorable current brought the ice floe near the opposite bank. The bird hopped off and reached home. We are all like this bird with the damaged wing. We are drifting here and there, unable to realize the formless supreme lord (paramēśhvara) who is without attributes (nirguṇa) and without form (nirākāra). By worshiping the God who is with qualities (saguṇa) and with form (sakāra), we realize īśhvara. The bird was able to get across when the formless water took the form of an ice floe.

Likewise, worshiping God with form and qualities helps us cross the ocean of worldly existence — the saṁsāra sāgara. The wind of God's grace will lead us to mōkṣha.

Sanātana Dharma is like a supermarket. Everything is available here. Sanātana Dharma proclaims that a human being is fundamentally God, and anyone can rise to that state of oneness with God through the right forms of spiritual practice.

12

Question: In the Hindu religion, it is not unusual for human beings to be worshiped as God. We do not see this to such an extent in other religions. Why is it so?

Amma: God resides in everyone. There is divinity within each one of us. Our svarūpa (essential nature) is the same as the svarūpa of God. Our ego hides God from us. When the veil of ego is removed, we become one with God. Many mahātmās who attained union with God have lived on this earth in all countries and in all ages. They have become one with God even while they were alive. Even so, there have been many more mahātmās and incarnations of God in Bhārat. This is why we see the practice of honoring and worshiping mahātmās to a greater extent in Bhārat. Also, the perspective that we are one with God can rarely be seen in other religions. This could also be a reason.

Usually, humans are totally identified with their physical bodies. This identification with the body is the ignorance or ajñāna that causes the ego to sprout. When the ego, the feeling of "I," is eradicated through right knowledge and surrender to God, we will realize the ātman, which is the real form, the svarūpa of God. We become one with God. When a mango matures and ripens, its sour and acerbic flavors become pure sweetness. Likewise, when our ignorance, i.e. our ego, is gone, then our selfishness and negative tendencies will fall away from us, and we will become sweet. From such a person, only good can happen to the world. When evil increases in this world, these mahātmās secure the harmony of this world to a certain extent. If we compare an ordinary human being to a ten- or twenty-watt bulb, the mahātmā can be compared to a bulb of a thousand watts or more. Being near and interacting with a mahātmā will influence us greatly. It strengthens good saṁskāras (tendencies) and weakens low and wicked saṁskāras in us. When we come out of an incense factory, our body will have the fragrance of incense. Association with a mahātmā can be compared to this.

Mahātmās know the supreme truth. If we follow their teachings and receive their blessings, our spiritual journey will be smooth. Through their blessings, we will gain all four puruṣhārthas, or goals of human endeavor. Great temples arise when the mahātmās awaken the divine energy of God in the stone of the idol. We can worship God in stone, clay, or any object. So, where is the shortcoming in worshiping mahātmās who have attained oneness with God? With the aim of realizing God, we have taken refuge in a mahātmā. The mahātmā then becomes our guru. When we move with self-surrender on the path advised by the guru, we will quickly attain self-realization. These are the reasons why we honor and worship mahātmās.

13

Question: In Sanātana Dharma, why is it said that the creator and creation are one?

Amma: Nothing in creation is separate from the creator. This is why we say that the creator and creation are one. God, the creator, manifests as and shines through his creations. It is the same divine consciousness that shines through the multitude of beings in this universe. This is the fundamental principle of the Hindu religion. Whatever the external differences, all objects and beings are fundamentally the same — all is God.

The spider weaves a web from the thread spun from within itself. It does not depend on any external source. Likewise, God created the universe from himself. When the spider has no more use of its web, it will pull it back into itself. Likewise, during the period of creation, God manifested the universe from himself. During the final dissolution, he will draw it back into himself. The dream and the creations in the dream are not separate from the dreamer. Likewise, it is God himself who has become his creation.

The dance originates from the dancer. The dancer exists before the dance, while the dance is happening, and after the dance. Likewise, only God exists before, during, and after creation. Sanātana Dharma says that there is nothing other than God.

The shape and use of gold earrings, chains, finger rings, and various other ornaments vary, but they are all gold. Likewise, all the objects in this world are fundamentally divine consciousness. They are brahman, the supreme reality. Because they are fundamentally one, we say that creation and creator are not two, but one. No one denies the outer differences. Whatever the differences in shape, nature, and characteristics, everything in this world is fundamentally the one divine consciousness.

We may ask, "If God created the world, who created God?" God has no cause. God is the primal cause, the non-dual, eternal, beginningless and endless consciousness and awareness.

14

Question: If creation and creator are one, why do we not see God's omnipotence and omniscience in cats, dogs, and other life forms?

Amma: When we say that the creator and creation are one, we only intend to state their fundamental oneness. External differences are never denied. Everything in creation is the manifest form of the creator. Nature is God in a manifest form. The real nature of each living being is one with God's true nature. It is pure consciousness or pure awareness. Therefore, there is no fundamental difference. This is the meaning behind the saying that the creator and creation are one. The difference is only in the upādhis, the instruments, through which the pure consciousness functions.

Many forms are made from the same clay: mud pots, human figurines, drinking jars, oil lamps, statues of horses, etc. Fundamentally, they are all clay. Likewise, we make knives, swords, needles, spades, pots, and other objects from the same iron. The names, forms, and uses of each are different. But fundamentally, they are all iron. Likewise, the fundamental substratum of this infinitely diverse world is God. The one God exists as the substratum of the infinitely varied abundance of this universe. The diversity of this universe is seen in the one God.

Imagine that many mirrors are spread out in the yard. The degree of dirt and dust on each mirror varies. All these mirrors will reflect the sun up in the sky. In the very dirty mirrors, we will see only a dull reflection of the sun. In the cleaner mirrors, we can see a clear reflection of the sun. Likewise, all living bodies are instruments reflecting the divine consciousness. God's power manifests differently according to the difference in the upādhis, the instruments. Suppose the same electric current flows through a hundred-watt and a thousand-watt bulb. The light emitted by the hundred-watt bulb will be significantly less than that of the thousand-watt bulb. Likewise, depending on the body-mind-intellect complex of individuals and other living beings, their abilities differ. A person's right eye can see very well, but the left eye does not have good vision. In this case, the left eye's vision is reduced because of problems besetting the left eye. Similarly, the magnitude with which the divine consciousness of God shines forth depends on the instruments. We can experience the same current as cold in refrigerators and heat in heaters. We see such diversity in this universe because of the differences between the upādhis, the instruments through which God shines forth.

15

Question: Kālī is portrayed as naked, wearing a garland of skulls, with weapons in her hands, and drinking blood. What is the meaning of worshiping such a Kālī?

Amma: Most Hindu gods, not just Kālī, are depicted as carrying different kinds of weapons in their hands. This does not mean that those gods kill humans. The asuras and rākṣhasas (two classes of demons) are symbols of the deeply imprinted negative tendencies and emotions of lust and desire, anger, envy, jealousy, etc., in the human mind. God annihilates these demonic qualities.

What is the inner meaning behind the reason why the Hindu gods hold weapons in their hands? Negative tendencies of the mind originate from ignorance. Kālī cuts asunder the rope of ignorance using the scimitar[3] of knowledge. She is not beheading human beings. Kālī is the one who destroys the ignorance inside us and grants us liberation. The severed head seen held in Kālī's hand is the head of the delusionary ego of "I." Liberation is the destruction of the feeling of "I."

Kālī never drinks human blood. She drinks the blood of desires, anger, etc., that infests the human mind. These tendencies arise from rajōguṇa, the quality of passion. The red blood signifies rajōguṇa. Kālī cuts asunder all the desires of the devotee who worships her and holds them close to her. She is so full of love. Only those who do not know this principle will say that Kālī drinks blood. Kālī also annihilates the tamōguṇa, the quality of dullness, which is the biggest obstacle to the destruction of the ego. Tamōguṇa is conquered by awakening the rajōguṇa that is conceived in dharma. This is the significance behind Kālī's fierce dance. We

[3] Short sword with curved blade.

are of two minds when we start to wake up in the morning. The lazy desire to keep lying in bed originates from tamōguṇa. But we have within us another bhāva, another emotion that cuts the head off this tamasic indolence and destroys it. It is then that we get up from bed. Kālī is the one who awakens this bhāva in us. If we consider it in this manner, we will realize that Kālī is the one who cuts off the heads of the qualities of tamas and rajas within us.

Kālī is the primal power behind the world's creation, sustenance and destruction. She destroys the sense of duality born of ignorance. The self-luminous and inherently perfect ātman shines forth when the feeling of duality disappears. We lose our identification with the physical body. This is the meaning behind Kālī's nakedness. Kālī is the perfect embodiment of expansiveness, love, and the qualities of motherhood. Kālī's dark color signifies infinity. Kālī is the kriyāśhakti, the power of action in this universe. Just as fire and its ability to burn are inseparable, Kālī standing with her foot placed on Śhiva's chest is the sign that Śhiva and Śhakti (the masculine and the feminine aspects of divinity) are inseparable from each other.

Kālī's eyes express both tenderness and fierceness. Kālī's fierceness is directed against the ego that distances her devotees from her. Her fierceness arises from the infinite love that she has for her devotees. The human skulls in Kālī's garland symbolize the ego in us. It is said that the ego is in the head. This is why people with huge egos never bow their heads in front of anyone. Kālī severs the heads, which are our egos, with her scimitar and wears them as a garland. This is the garland of skulls around her neck. Kālī is the embodiment of love who destroys our egos and liberates us. She blesses us and grants us refuge.

16

Question: Some people say that Gaṇēśha with his elephant head and human body is an illogical myth. What is Amma's response to this?

Amma: We find it illogical only when we consider Gaṇēśha as a human being with an elephant head. God has no particular form, but he can take on any form to bless devotees.

Gaṇēśha is the īśhvara-bhāva that blesses us with the ability to overcome challenges and obstacles. At the beginning of creation, there was the praṇava — the sound of ōm. Gaṇēśha is of the form of praṇava. Because of this reason, and because he removes all obstacles when we perform our dharmic actions, we worship Gaṇēśha first before starting any important venture. Elephants fling away anything that obstructs their path with their trunks, or they will destroy it with their tusks or legs and thus move ahead. Gaṇēśha reminds us to break through all obstacles with effort and willpower. The elephant is the biggest animal on land, and it signifies samaṣhṭi, the whole, while the body of a human being signifies vyaṣhṭi, the individual. Fundamentally, the individual and the whole are one. Therefore, an individual can rise up to the level of God-consciousness — īśhvara-bhāva. The obstacles to this are our asuric (demonic) tendencies. Gaṇēśha is the one who conquers them. The gaṇas (a class of celestial beings) are the primal powers of this universe. As Gaṇēśha[4] is the lord of the forces of the universe, he can remove every obstacle. We can also say that the gaṇas are good

---

[4] Gaṇēśha is a combination of two words, 'gaṇa' + 'īśha;' 'gaṇa' refers to a class of celestial beings who are associated with governing the universe, and 'īśha' means lord.

and noble thoughts. If our thoughts are noble and benevolent, it is easy to succeed in any venture.

The elephant head signifies the qualities needed to succeed in our efforts. The elephant's trunk can lift up the heaviest and the minutest object. Likewise, we should be able to grasp obvious and subtle matters. The elephant is always aware, so its ears can pick up the slightest sound. This shows us that we should always remain alert and attentive without a moment's lapse. Gaṇēśha's big stomach signifies that he holds the entire universe within him. His four arms indicate his lordship over the four directions. We see a rope, an ax, a lotus, and a sweet in Gaṇēśha's hands. One hand shows the abhayamudrā, a gesture of protection that dispels the fear in devotees. The ax represents the power of discernment that cuts through rāga and dvēṣha, the likes and dislikes that bind humanity. Then we are bound to God with the rope of love. The lotus flower has the most balanced and perfect shape. Therefore, it signifies perfection and self-realization. When the lotus of the heart blossoms, the jīva unites with īśhvara. Gaṇēśha bestows sweets that signify happiness to his devotees. Gaṇēśha's vehicle, the mouse, is a symbol of our mind. Our mind is fickle, like the mouse that is always in motion. The message given by the mouse sitting still and gazing at Gaṇēśha is to turn our mind inward to God. Almost all Hindus worship Gaṇēśha.

There are many Puranic stories about Gaṇēśha. These stories have deep inner meanings. Each one is meant to awaken good qualities in us and help us understand the right principles. We need to accept them only if they align with science, logic, and our experiences.

Bhārat's real wealth is its saṁskāra, its noble culture. We should try to understand and accept it. Nowadays, our faith is relegated to rituals and festivals. We have little knowledge of our culture's fundamental principles. Our faith is not strong enough to withstand even the slightest criticism. Because of our ignorance, we can only stand and listen to others criticize our various conceptualizations of God. Our faith must be as strong and sure as Prahlāda's[5]. We should be

---

[5] Infuriated by Prahlāda's unconditional faith in Lord Viṣhṇu, the demon king Hiraṇyakaśhipu tried various ways to torture and even kill the young boy, who was his own son. But Prahlāda remained steadfast in his faith and finally, the Lord incarnated as the man-lion

able to imbibe the foundation of our saṁskāra explained in our scriptural texts.

17

Question: Some people consider the śhivaliṅga as indecent. Is there any foundation for this?

Amma: Children, they say this because they have yet to understand the correct principle of the śhivaliṅga. Each person makes judgements of good or bad based on their mental saṁskāra (conditioning).

Every religion and organization has their own unique symbols. The cloth used to make the flag of a nation or a political party may cost only ten rupees, but think of the great value we give to it. People see in the flag a nation or a political party. For the party members, the flag is a symbol of their ideals. Suppose a person says that this cloth only costs ten rupees and tears it up or spits on it. It will definitely lead to a major confrontation. When they see the flag, no one thinks that it is made of cotton, or that manure is used to fertilize cotton and that manure stinks. Instead, in the

---

Narasiṁha to protect his devotee and kill the wicked king.

flag, the party members see their party and its ideals.

For Christians, the cross is a symbol of sacrifice. When they stand in front of the cross and pray, they do not think that it is the means by which convicts were crucified. They see the cross as the symbol of Christ's mercy and sacrifice. When Muslim children prostrate in the direction of Mecca, they are thinking of God's qualities. Why is it that only the depictions and physical representations of Hindu gods are denigrated by some people? When a son sees the portrait of his father, he does not remember the paint that is used nor the painter. He remembers his father.

The śhivaliṅga is not the symbol of any particular religion. It encompasses a scientific principle.

Numerous signs and symbols, such as symbols for multiplication and division, are used in mathematics and science. Doesn't every religion and every country use these symbols? Does anyone reject them after finding out which religion's followers invented these signs? Everyone who studies mathematics accepts those signs and symbols. Likewise, none who seek the truth can denounce the śhivaliṅga once they understand the principle behind it.

Children, liṅga means exalted place. The liṅga is that from which the universe originated and into which it will finally merge back. The great seers of ancient times, the ṛiṣhis, sought to find out how this universe began and, through their intense meditation, discovered that the beginning and substratum of all is brahman. Brahman cannot be described in words. It cannot be pointed out. The beginning and end of all is in brahman. It is without qualities (nirguṇa) as it is the seat of all qualities. It is formless (nirākāra). How can you describe something that is without any qualities or attributes? The mind and sense-organs can comprehend only that which is with qualities (saguṇa).

At the critical juncture between brahman and the beginning of creation, the sages discovered the symbol of the śhivaliṅga. It denotes the creation of the universe from brahman. The śhivaliṅga is the symbol by which the great ṛiṣhis revealed their experiential knowledge of the truth to ordinary people. The supreme truth is nirguṇa, without any qualities or attributes. It transcends name, form, and attributes. Hence, the sages envisioned the scientific symbol of the śhivaliṅga to meditate on and worship this truth.

Scientists who research rays invisible to the naked eye use symbols to explain them to others. For example, an x-ray denotes a particular kind of ray. Likewise, when we hear "śhivaliṅga," we understand that it is the saguṇa form of the nirguṇa brahman.

The sound "Śhiva" also means "mangalam — auspicious." The sound "mangalam" does not have a form of its own. By worshiping the śhivaliṅga, the symbol of auspiciousness, one attains auspiciousness. Auspiciousness has no caste or creed. Knowing its true principle, anyone who worships the śhivaliṅga will attain auspiciousness.

At the beginning of creation, the supreme truth separated into two as prakṛiti and puruṣha. Here, the term puruṣha does not denote men, it denotes the pure consciousness that dwells within the ātman — the ātmā-chaitanya. By the term prakṛiti, the sages meant the universe we experience and understand. Puruṣha and prakṛiti are not two. They are one, like fire and its power to burn. They cannot be separated. For someone unfamiliar with spiritual terms, the word puruṣha will only mean men. Therefore, the sages envisioned a male form for the paramātman, the supreme self that is pure consciousness, and named him Śhiva. Prakṛiti was envisioned as female and called Śhakti and Dēvī. There will be a motionless base behind every movement — like the motionless stone mortar and the long pestle that does the pounding, or like the grinding stone that acts as the motionless base and the small pestle that does the grinding. Likewise, Śhiva is the motionless or changeless principle for all the movements in this universe. Prakṛiti is the force responsible for movement or change. When we meditate with single-minded focus on the śhivaliṅga, the symbol of the unity of Śhiva and Śhakti, the supreme truth will awaken within us.

We may wonder why the śhivaliṅga was envisioned in this particular shape. Scientists now say that the universe is egg-shaped. The egg is called aṇḍa. For thousands of years in Bhārat, the word used to denote the universe was brahmāṇḍa[6]. Brahman means that which is the biggest. The śhivaliṅga is a smaller version of this egg-shaped universe. When we worship the śhivaliṅga, we are

[6] Comprising 'brahma' (the vast, the absolute) and 'aṇḍa' (egg).

in fact, seeing and worshiping the entire universe as auspicious, pure consciousness. Its principle is not about worshiping a God residing above the heavens. The śhivaliṅga teaches us to see as the worship of Śhiva, the acts of selfless service we perform for the welfare of this universe, which includes humanity and other living beings.

Currently, we are like small chicks enclosed within the eggshell of our ego. A small chick can only dream of the freedom of the sky. It cannot experience it. For a baby bird to eventually fly high, the mother bird first has to incubate the eggs with her warmth so that they hatch. Likewise, to experience the blissful self, the eggshell that is our ego has to break. The śhivaliṅga, in the shape of an egg, will help to awaken this awareness in the mind of the spiritual practitioner.

When we sing, "ākāśha-liṅga pāhi mām, ātmā-liṅga pāhi mām," we are praying that, "May God who is as omnipresent as the sky protect us. May God who is the supreme self, who is our true nature, protect us."[7] Not even fools will pray to a body part of a human being to protect them.

---

[7] From the Sanskrit bhajan *Parama Śhiva Mām Pāhi.*

What is the advantage of ridiculing a divine symbol millions have worshiped for thousands of years to gain self-realization? What good does it do to insinuate a meaning that it does not have? It will only cause anger and hatred.

The Purānic tales tell us that Śhiva burnt Kāmadēva, the God of desire, to ashes with his third eye. Now we consider all that is of this material world to be the truth, eternal, and our own. Our eyes can only see this. Only if the third eye of knowledge opens is it possible for us to see that all this is perishable and that only the divine consciousness residing within us is eternal. Only then will we experience the supreme bliss. Then there is no difference between man and woman, mine and yours. This is the destruction of Kāma. The śhivaliṅga helps us to grasp this truth and liberate our minds from desire. This is why it is worshiped equally by man, woman, chaṇḍāla[8], brahmin, the old, and the young. Only a mind deluded by lust can see the śhivaliṅga as a symbol of lust. We should try to purify the minds of such people by explaining the fundamental principle behind the śhivaliṅga.

---

[8] An outcast.

The śhivaliṅga shows us that Śhiva and Śhakti are not two but one. This is relevant in family life also. The husband and wife should be of one mind. If the man is the home's foundation, the woman is the strength and energy. It is doubtful whether any other symbol reveals the equality and love between man and woman with such clarity. This is another reason why Amma has given such importance to the śhivaliṅga in the Brahmasthānam temples she has consecrated.

18

Question: Śhiva is depicted wearing serpents as ornaments. What does this symbolize?

Amma: The serpent is said to symbolize the kuṇḍalinī śhakti (spiritual energy located at the base of the spine). The serpent is also said to symbolize kāma (desire). It indicates the different aspects of the same śhakti (primordial power). When our strength and power are directed outward and used to fulfill worldly desires, it becomes kāma. It is the poison that drains our inner energy. If snake venom is used therapeutically, it is medicine; it is an antidote to poison. Likewise, when we turn our strength and power inward through sādhanā (disciplined and focused spiritual practice) and search for God, the dormant spiritual energy located at the base of the spine awakens as the kuṇḍalinī śhakti and moves upward to reach the state of oneness with the divine. Thus, the sādhak (spiritual seeker) attains immortality. Śhiva wears the snake as an ornament around his neck to symbolize complete control over kāma, all forms of desire.

19

Question: What does it mean when it's said that Śhiva lives in the cremation grounds?

Amma: Desire is the reason for a human being's sorrow. The thought that one is not complete or perfect is the reason why the mind rushes from one desire to another. One can never attain perfect peace if one concentrates solely on achieving worldly gains. All the worldly desires of a human being, along with his physical body, will be burnt to ashes in the cremation ground. Śhiva is the one who dances blissfully there. This is why it is said that Śhiva resides in the cremation grounds. This does not mean that bliss is experienced after death. Everything is within us. We and the universe are one; both are equally whole and perfect. When attachment to the body is burnt in the fire of knowledge, bliss naturally overwhelms us. This is where Śhiva resides. He is adorned with ash from the burning pyres. This represents victory over every desire. When we put sacred ash[9] on our forehead, we receive its medicinal benefits and remember the body's temporal nature. It reminds us that this body will soon cease to be and motivates us to do as much good as we can, as fast as possible, before it is destroyed.

Śhiva is called vairāgī, the dispassionate one. When we hear the word vairāgya (dispassion), we may consider it to mean dislike of the world. But that is not the meaning. It means without attachment. Grownups do not attach the same importance to toys as children do. Likewise, vairāgya means not giving excessive value to power and position, the comforts of the body, friends and relatives, etc. If we do not develop the right vairāgya, our happiness will depend on the words and opinions of others. Our life will become a toy in another's hands. Vairāgya gives

---

[9] Typically known as *bhasma* or *vibhūti*, traditionally made of dried cow dung that is burned to ashes.

us true freedom. If we gain vairāgya, no object of the world can veil our natural joy. Śhiva, adorned with ash, living in the cremation grounds, teaches us this principle. This is why Śhiva is the ādiguru — the original or first guru.

20

Question: What is māyā? How can we overcome it?

Amma: Māyā is that which veils the truth and leads us away from it. It can never give us enduring peace. We chase after objects and experiences of this world, believing them to be the truth. Thus, we move away from the truth. We lose enduring, eternal peace. For a dreamer, the dream world is true. But when he wakes up, he realizes it is not the truth. Likewise, we are now in a dream caused by māyā. We will know the nature of truth only if we wake up from our dreams.

We experience this physical world, made of the five great elements, through our five jñānēndriyas — organs of perception: the eyes, the nose, the tongue, the ears, and the skin. But the truth is that whatever we comprehend with our sense organs can never give us lasting peace. Because they are like the objects in our dreams, they are mithyā, which means that they are constantly changing. Therefore, the joy and sorrow we believe we experience through them will be short-lived. Not understanding this, we chase after worldly pleasures again and again. We do not know that sorrow hides behind every experience of joy. This is māyā.

Once, two vultures went hunting for prey, and they caught a snake and a rat. Both vultures came and perched near each other on the branches of a pipal tree. When the snake saw the rat, it stretched its neck towards it. The rat curled itself up inside the vulture's talons for safety. Both of them forgot that they were already in death's hands. This is the wonder of māyā. Likewise, even when each moment we are living in the shadow of death, we also forget this, getting caught in the clutches of likes and dislikes.

Māyā is the main reason for the joy and sorrow that we now experience in our lives. Often, we lose courage and become despondent, mistaking what was not there to be there, and what did not happen to have happened. This occurs when our strong attachments to or aversions against people and objects prevent us from seeing reality. This is why we say that people who travel on the path of spirituality should shed their likes and dislikes. When we discern and understand the difference between the eternal and the temporal, we will realize that this temporal world is in itself māyā. Māyā will not affect us if, like the honey bee that sucks only the nectar from flowers, we live imbibing only the world's goodness.

While traveling through a dark forest, sometimes people mistake a thorn pricking their foot for a snake bite. They start crying out in panic and exhibit all the symptoms of a snake bite. Until the viṣhavaidya, the traditional snake bite healer, comes, examines, and affirms that it is only a thorn prick, they will experience the fear of death. Likewise, often in life, we wrongly assume that which is not to be, to be there, and that which did not happen to have occurred. This will drain all courage and energy from us. This happens when we lose the ability to see the reality due to our excessive attachment to or aversion to people and objects.

We have misconceptions about objects because we have wrong perceptions about them. We become selfishly attached to individuals and objects. Because of our selfish attachments, we experience sorrow and suffering. Deluded by māyā, we mistake the truth to be untruth and untruth to be the truth. If this world is māyā, what should our approach be? Should we reject it? Not at all. If we approach the world and its objects with wise discernment, they will guide us to the truth. Instead of being beguiled by the world's objects, we should seek the changeless truth which is the foundation of this world. Each life experience should be seen as an opportunity to seek that immutable truth. Then we will be able to find goodness in everything. Joy and sorrow will become lessons for us to learn from. We will experience the same illusory universe that veils the truth, now illumining and revealing the truth.

While walking on the thin barrier between paddy fields, if we slip and our leg becomes completely covered with mud, we will consider it dirt and wash our leg clean at once. But when a potter came that way and saw the mud, he thought about its uses. He understood that the mud was perfect for making pots and made many pots out of it. It was not dirt for the potter. A woman who went to collect firewood from the forest found a stone. She started using it as a grinding stone. But a sculptor saw the same stone and understood its pure quality. He bought the stone, made a sculpture from it, and enshrined it in a temple. He offered fruits and precious stones and worshipped it. Until its greatness was discovered, it remained just a stone. We can use fire to cook and also to burn down a house. A doctor uses a knife to perform surgery and save the patient, while a knife is a lethal weapon in the hands of a murderer. Therefore, instead of dismissing everything as māyā, we should understand the true nature of each object and use it well, rejecting only its negative aspects.

The great sages saw only good in this world. The world is saved by those who know māya. Māyā will never subjugate them. However, those who do not understand māyā destroy themselves and become a burden to others. If we can move forward seeing only the good aspects of everything, then there is nothing for us to reject. We will be able to accept everything as different forms and bhāvas of the supreme truth.

21

Question: Does the Hindu religion reject materialism?

Amma: The Hindu religion does not see materialism and spirituality as being at odds with each other. It does not reject materialism or worldly life in the name of spirituality. On the contrary, if we imbibe spirituality, we will find it easier to face the challenges posed by worldly life. Life will become meaningful by having awareness of the goal. The ancient sages, the ṛiṣhis, built up the material sciences and the various art forms on the foundation of spirituality. They saw even these as stepping stones towards realizing the supreme truth and created and designed them in a manner which would finally lead to God.

Thus, many branches of science became highly developed in Bhārat: bhāṣha śhāstra — philology; tachchu śhāstra — carpentry; vastu śhāstra — architecture; jyōtiṣha śhāstra — astrology; gaṇita śhāstra — mathematics; ārōgya śhāstra — health and medical sciences; artha śhāstra — statecraft, political science, and economics; nāṭya śhāstra — science of drama; saṅgīta śhāstra — the science of music; kāma śhāstra — science of desire; nāḍi śhāstra — a form of astrology; tarka śhāstra — the philosophy of dialectics, logic, and reasoning.

Countless branches of science have been developed and expanded in this land. Sanātana

Dharma nurtures and nourishes each field and facet of human life and culture. Thus, it encompasses the various states of human life and uplifts us.

22

Question: Does Amma recognize the various traditions and rituals of the Hindu religion?

Amma: Amma honors every ritual and tradition that allows us to reach the goal. Children, you may ask, does Amma need to do so? This world is not separate from God; they are not two. God and his devotee are not separate from each other. Thus, we see unity in diversity. Even though Amma knows that God is not separate from her, Amma bows down before everyone. Even though Amma knows that both the terrace and the staircase leading up to the terrace are built of the same material, Amma cannot reject the staircase. We should not forget the path we have traveled. A child comes down with jaundice. It cannot have salt as it will aggravate the disease. But he does not like food without salt. If he sees regular salted food, he will take it and eat it. Knowing this, the mother does not add salt to any food she cooks.

Even though the others are not sick, they will also forfeit salt for the child's sake. Likewise, even though Amma doesn't need to follow traditions and rituals, Amma does so to become a model for her children.

The goal of all traditions and rituals is to sustain dharma. The habits, actions, and behaviors that nourish dharma gradually evolve into traditions. Over time, people forget the goal behind the tradition and it becomes a mere ritual without helping to protect dharma. Then āchāras (traditions) become anāchāras (wrong customs and practices). In such situations, it is necessary to change and progress with the times.

23

Question: Do we need to believe in God to become a Hindu?

Amma: The principles of Sanātana Dharma are the priceless treasure given to this world by the selfless sages, the ṛiṣhis of ancient Bhārat. These principles are as indispensable for anyone seeking peace as air and water are for life. Sanātana Dharma does not ask us to believe in a God sitting somewhere up in the heavens. It says, "Believe in yourself. Everything is within you."

Sanātana Dharma does not require us to believe these words unquestioningly. It asks us to travel on the path laid down by the scriptures and the words of the gurus, and thus to seek out and directly experience the truth. The strength of the atomic bomb, capable of reducing this world to ashes, lies in the tiny atom. The pipal tree that grows tall and wide, spreading its roots across a vast area, grew from a single tiny seed. Likewise, the power of God, which is the foundation of this world, resides in each one of us. This can be understood through logic, and experienced and realized through sādhanā, systematic spiritual practice. It is enough to follow and practice the ways in which to awaken this power with focus and faith. Sanātana Dharma does not ask you to believe in God. It tells you to believe in yourself. This is because God resides within ourselves. Fundamentally, we are of the nature of God.

24

Question: Where is the need for faith in God in human life?

Amma: We can also live without faith in God. But when faced with crises, we must depend on and take refuge in God to move forward with firm, unfaltering steps. We should be ready to follow God's path. Man's abilities are limited. When human beings face many problems, one after the other, they become aware of their helplessness. If we have faith in an all-powerful God, we can move forward even then without faltering.

A life without faith in God can be compared to an argument with only two lawyers present. The argument will go nowhere. A judge is essential to pronounce judgment. A judgment will not be delivered if the argument continues without the judge. Only through God can we find the answers to many problems and difficulties in life.

We worship God so that divine qualities grow in us. If we can imbibe those qualities by other means, then we do not need any particular belief. But whether we believe or not, God is an everlasting truth. This truth will not be affected in the least, whether we believe it or not. The gravitational pull of the earth is a reality. Just because we do not believe in it or acknowledge it, will not make it cease to be. An accident will happen if we reject gravity and jump from high up. Then we will be forced to acknowledge and accept this truth. Likewise, turning our heads away from reality is like closing our eyes and making everything dark. When we believe in this universal power, God, and build our lives by acknowledging this truth, we can lead a life free of distress. When we say that God does not exist, it is like negating the existence of the tongue while speaking with the tongue.

25

Question: Is there anyone unfit or ineligible to follow the Hindu religion?

Amma: Sanātana Dharma does not reject anyone, no one is regarded as unfit or ineligible. Keeping someone away from spirituality by saying that they are not eligible can be compared to building a hospital and deciding that there is no need for patients. Even a watch that has stopped working will show the time correctly twice a day. Therefore, we need to have acceptance towards others. When we reject others by saying, "You are not good enough, you are not good enough," it will make them vengeful and animal instincts will arise in them. They will fall further into wrongdoing. However, if we praise the goodness in someone and try to correct his wickedness with patience and love, we will be able to uplift him.

Human beings commit wrongs because they are ignorant of who they really are. Therefore, Sanātana Dharma tells us not to reject anyone but to provide them with the right knowledge. If the sages had kept Ratnākara at a distance, saying he was a forest hunter and a robber and hence unworthy, he would not have transformed into sage Vālmīki. Sanātana Dharma shows us that even a cruel thief can become a mahātmā.

If a precious jewel was found lying in excrement, no one would abandon it. They would clean away the excrement and try to make the jewel their own. Likewise, we cannot reject anyone, since divine consciousness dwells within all. We should be able to see God in everyone without seeing any difference between the great and the insignificant. For this, we first need to clean the impurities that cloud our minds.

26

Question: What is meant by surrendering or offering to God?

Amma: When we say īśhvara samarpaṇam (surrendering or offering to God), some people think we will get the desired result only if we offer something to God. This is not how we should understand the word samarpaṇam. At present, we are in the realm of the mind and intellect: "I am the physical body. I am the son or daughter of such and such a person. This is my name..." Like this, we have to relinquish all that we have added to the "I."

Ego! This is our only creation, and it is we who have to relinquish it. This is what we have to surrender or offer to God. If we surrender the ego, then everything transforms into God's creation. We will become a flute on God's lips. We will become a conch from which the ōm-sound arises. In order to awaken to this all-pervasive energy, all we need to do is to relinquish our individual minds, which are our own creations. If we let go of "me and mine," then there is no individual — there is only totality.

The seed in hand will not germinate, and if we throw it on a rock, it will not germinate. It will have to be thrown into the earth. Likewise, we must relinquish our ego to get the right result for any of our actions. We should develop humility.

We should develop an attitude of surrender. Then everything becomes possible with God's grace.

We should surrender our minds to God. But it is not possible to take the mind and offer it to God. Hence, offering whatever the mind is attached to becomes equal to offering our minds. Some people love sweet pudding. So, they offer it as naivēdyam, food given to the Lord. It becomes of benefit when some ten poor kids get to savor it as prasād. The mind is most attached to wealth. To gain release from this attachment, money is given as an offering.

When we go to the temple, we give pușhpāñjali (flower offerings) to God. In reality, we should offer the flower of our heart. Real devotion is when we are able to offer our hearts to the Lord. This is real surrender. As a symbol of this surrender, we offer flowers.

We should gain the attitude "I am nothing, you are everything" by surrendering to God. Then there will be no more "I" – everything will become the Lord. This is the total destruction of selfishness. Our words, thoughts, and actions will not be for our comfort; they will be aimed at the world's welfare. This is because such a devotee does not see anything in this world as separate from God. The total destruction of the ego is the aim behind our surrender to God.

27

Question: Ghee, honey, and other substances are sacrificed into the fire during a hōma to please God. Is it correct to waste them? It is said that many other objects of value are also sacrificed in the fire. What is Amma's opinion on this?

Amma: Amma does not agree with sacrificing costly objects into the fire. If it were done, it may be to get rid of the mind's attachment to those objects. Even so, it is better to donate rather than sacrifice them to the sacred fire. This will benefit the poor. Amma considers this to be the more rational approach.

A hōma has many subtle layers of meaning. In essence, it is our ego that we should offer as a sacrifice to God. The ego is the mind's creation. The hōma symbolizes the offering of our minds to God. Therefore, the oblations we offer to the fire symbolize the worldly objects to which our mind is attached. However, a hōma in which numerous oblations are offered to the fire is not the only way to please God. It is enough to perform good actions. If we have a mind that loves and serves others, it is enough – grace will reach us.

When we offer oblations to the fire, we cannot categorically say they are being wasted. Nature also benefits from the hōma rituals, which are precepts found in the ritualistic portion of the *Vēdas.* A few of its benefits have been scientifically proven. The smoke arising from the fire when ghee, sesame seeds, karuka grass, coconut, and honey are offered to it purifies the atmosphere. Thus, germs in the air can be destroyed without using poisonous chemicals. We also benefit from breathing in the fragrant air.

When we get up early in the morning, light the fire in the sacrificial fire pit, sit with good posture, erect with legs crossed, and perform the hōma rituals, it focuses our attention and makes it one-pointed, reducing tension. We perspire when we sit near the fire and the body is cleansed of all impurities. We breathe in the fragrance of burning ghee and coconut. This is good for our health. Along with it, our minds and the atmosphere are also purified. We can see that every traditional ritual prescribed by our ancestors was also intended to sustain the harmony of the universe – no ritual ever polluted nature.

In most homes, it was the practice to light an oil lamp at dusk. When oil is poured into a brass lamp and the wick is lit, it also purifies the atmosphere. Amma has heard that the smoke emanating from the lit lamp is collected in a small pot. After giving birth, women mix the soot collected from this smoke with lemon juice and line their eyelids with it. This destroys the germs on the eyelids, and there are no side effects. This smoke is different from kerosene smoke. All the traditions of the past benefited nature. In the early days, fire was made by using araṇī, wooden sticks that are rubbed against each other to kindle fire by friction. Unlike matchsticks, this method does not pollute the atmosphere.

Years ago, when children were vaccinated, mothers would smear the wound with cow dung so that it would heal well. But now, if we apply cow dung to a wound, it will turn septic. Cow dung is now highly impure. The medicine of yesteryear has become a poison now. In those days, farmers did not spray chemical fertilizers and pesticides on their farmland. Dry leaves and cow dung were the only fertilizers. Today, farming is done with poisonous pesticides and fertilizers. Hay from these fields is used to feed the cows. The cow dung of such cows may contain traces of poisonous chemicals. Even if such cow dung touches a wound, it becomes septic. Nature has become so very polluted.

Amma does not negate the fact that use of these chemicals has brought in financial gain. By using them, temporarily, we get better harvests. But in another way, they are killing us. When we say that better yields are a solution to starvation, we are forgetting the fact that by eating the grains and vegetables produced by using these fertilizers, many cells in our body are being destroyed. We become chronic patients. We are not very bothered by a single needle prick. But if we are pricked relentlessly it will end in our death! Similar is the effect when poisonous chemical fertilizers enter our body. Our cells are dying one by one. We will realize the gravity of the problem only when we fall dead. We are feeding on different poisons through air, water, and food. They are turning us into patients and leading us to our death.

Today, we don't understand the inherent ill effects of many of our practices in the name of cleanliness. Don't we use disinfectants to clean dirty rooms and kill germs? Even breathing in the fragrance of these disinfectants is dangerous to our health. They kill even the bacteria that are good for humanity. When we perform a hōma, it kills dangerous bacteria and purifies the atmosphere. Traditionally, only items that would purify the atmosphere were offered into the fire. None of them were harmful.

Nowadays, we use chemicals to kill ants. It is poison that we should not breathe in. It kills not only ants but the cells in our body. But, when we are breathing in the fragrant smoke arising from the hōma, it energizes and rejuvenates the cells in our body. It is beneficial not only for humanity but for nature also.

In earlier days, castor oil was given to purge the stomach without harming the body. But today, people take many different medications for this, which not only cause loose motion but also kill many beneficial bacteria within the body. Even knowing this, for the sake of ease and comfort, many people depend on such pills. We only care for temporary ease; we do not bother about future implications. Our ancestors performed each action with a wholesome and comprehensive vision of nature. Hōma was also envisaged with this perspective. Even so, Amma will not say that everyone should perform hōma now. It is enough to use the money that would have been spent on hōma for charitable activities and donations. Also, plant the saplings of ten trees. This will benefit the atmosphere and protect nature.

28

Question: If God is everywhere, then why do we need temples?

Amma: Sanātana Dharma has a unique distinction: it meets everyone at their own level and uplifts them from where they stand. People come from different saṁskāras – cultures and backgrounds. They should be guided according to their saṁskāra. If a child feeding on breast milk is given meat to eat, it will not be able to digest it. We should give it food that it can digest. Some patients are allergic to injections, so they need to take tablets. Likewise, we should consider everyone's mental and physical aptitude and advise them on a path aligned with their saṁskāra. This is why different sampradāyas – spiritual traditions with their own doctrines and practices – came into being. This is how the concepts of God with form and attributes (saguṇa) and without form and attributes (nirguṇa), as well as the paths of bhakti yōga, karma yōga, etc., came into being.

Fundamentally, they all focus on the discernment between the eternal and the temporal, called nitya-anitya vivēka. Know with your discerning intellect what is changeless and what keeps constantly changing, and attain the changeless eternal. Archana, pūjā, and bhajans all aim to achieve this goal. We need braille to teach letters to a child who has no sight. We need sign language for a child who cannot hear. We should guide each person from the level where they currently stand. To go to the level of ordinary human beings and uplift them, temples are necessary. We cannot reject them.

The wind is everywhere, but isn't it felt more under a fan? If we sit under a tree, we feel coolness like nowhere else as we experience a breeze's freshness and pleasant comfort. Likewise, when we worship God through an upādhi (instrument), we will be able to experience God's presence with more intensity. There is milk in the cow, but we will not get milk if we tweak its ears. We receive milk only when we squeeze its udder. Likewise, even though God is everywhere, his divine presence can be felt more easily in temples for those who believe in temple worship. We need faith to experience this. Faith is the mind's tuning. Even though the presence of God is palpable in temples, those without faith will not be able to experience it. Faith provides the experience of the divine presence. Sunlight is everywhere, but for its light to enter a closed room, we need to open the doors. Likewise, we will be able to experience the presence of God only if we open the doors of our hearts.

Once, Amma was watching a dance program with the Amritapuri āśhram residents. A Western couple held hands while performing their traditional dance forms. One of Amma's daughters did not like this. She said, "Oh! What is this? A man and a woman dancing together?" Amma asked her, "Would you feel such shame if it were Śhiva and Pārvatī dancing together?" Because we see their dance as divine, we do not have any problems with it. When we utter the words Śhiva and Pārvatī, we feel their divinity. We have faith in them, and therefore see their dance as pure. Because we are unable to see divinity in that man and woman, we find their dance embarrassing. Our mind and mental attitudes are most important. Likewise, if we move forward with unshakeable faith, God will become an experience for us. Faith is the foundation.

Numerous devotees have gained the experience of God through temple worship. Temples create an unparalleled atmosphere as people gather in them to pray together with one heart. Such an aura is not present in other places. An office does not have the same ambience as a liquor bar, and a liquor bar does not have the ambience of a temple. While mental health is lost in a bar, it is gained in a temple. Temples are suffused with noble thought waves. They help to soothe the troubled, anxious, and stressed mind. There is a unique feature to a perfume factory. Upon entering, we will feel a pleasant fragrance that fills the entire factory. In contrast, a chemical factory will have an unpleasant odor. The pure atmosphere of a temple, intense with devotion, will make the mind one-pointed and help to awaken the mood of devotion, bhakti bhāva, within us. Temples are akin to mirrors. We look in the mirror and clean the dirt from our faces. Likewise, through temple worship, we should clean the impurities of the mind. Then within our pure hearts, we will see and experience God. This is the real goal of temple worship.

29

Question: Through temple worship, aren't we limiting the omnipresent God to a single idol?

Amma: Temples help the limited human being experience the limitless God. Even if we are surrounded by water, we need to use a pot or a cup to collect and drink it. We need an upādhi – a means, an instrument. Temples are places where God, the all-pervading, is given a place and a form and worshiped as prescribed in the scriptural texts. Temple worship is one of the initial stages of worshiping God. The temple and the physical form of the idol enshrined within the temple help us to establish and strengthen our connection to God through worship. Gradually, we should gain the ability to perceive divine consciousness everywhere. Through proper temple worship, we gain this ability. This is the goal of temple worship. When children are very young, we show them pictures of parrots and starlings and teach them, "This is a parrot, this is a starling." When they grow up, they do not need the pictures of a parrot or starling to recognize them. But in the beginning, it was necessary. In reality, everything is God. There is nothing to reject. The steps to the top floor of a house and the top floor are made of the same metal and cement. But we understood this only after we reached the top. But to reach there, we needed the steps. The benefits of temples are similar.

We say that we can be born in a temple, but we shouldn't die in a temple. The temple can be an upādhi, an instrument in our search for God, but we should not remain attached to it. Perfect freedom is the release from all attachments. We should not think that God is limited to his vigrahas (idols). Everything is divine energy, pure consciousness. Nothing is inert matter. Through temple worship, we should gain the attitude to see everything as divine consciousness, and to love and serve. It is an attitude of total acceptance. We should know that we, as well as everything around us, are God. We should develop an attitude of seeing everything as one, as one self. How can we hate anything if we are able to see everything as God? Temples and their rituals aim to guide individuals towards this level of oneness.

We may think that the ocean and its waves are two, but both are water. We may think that the gold chain, bangle, finger ring, and anklet are all different; they are worn on different parts of the body. But they are all gold. At the level of gold, they are all one; there is no difference at all. But if we look at their external forms, they are different. Likewise, even though we find seemingly diverse forms all around, in principle, they are all one — brahman. Only the one exists. The goal of human life is to know this through direct experience. When a human being knows this, all their problems end. It can be compared to the night disappearing when the sun rises. Scientists tell us now that all is energy. But the ṛiṣhis have gone one step further and proclaimed that all is divine consciousness: "sarvaṁ brahmamayaṁ." This was their direct experience.

To realize this, we must move on from the belief that God exists only in the idols enshrined in the temples. We should be able to see the divine consciousness in everything. To achieve this, we should perform temple worship with the knowledge of the ultimate oneness of everything. Indeed, we should worship the divine consciousness that dwells within our own self. But because it is difficult for ordinary human beings to do so, this divine consciousness is seen in the idol enshrined in the temple, like a reflection in a mirror.

Through temple worship, we should build a temple within ourselves. Then we will be able to see God anywhere. This should be the goal when we go to pray before the idol inside the temple. When we stand before the sanctum sanctorum and behold the idol of the Lord within the shrine, we should close our eyes and see within our hearts the form of the Lord that we saw enshrined outside. When we open our eyes, we should see God in everything around us. Similarly, as we go beyond all forms, we can realize the all-pervading supreme self that dwells within us. The temple and the idol enshrined within help us reach a state of fulfillment.

30

Question: What is the need for making oblations in temples?

Amma: God does not need anything from us. He is the Lord of this universe; there is nothing that he lacks. Why should the sun need a candle?

The real offering to God is to understand and live with the right knowledge of the fundamental principles. Eat for your needs, sleep for your needs, and speak only when you need to; do not waste time needlessly; take good care of the elderly, say good words to them; help children to learn; and keep aside a small portion of your income to serve the poor — all these are prayers to God. When we bring the right awareness to our thoughts, words, and deeds, life itself becomes an act of worship. This is the right offering. However, we cannot understand matters this way because we have not learned the scriptural texts properly. Now, there are not enough opportunities to understand Sanātana Dharma. There are many temples and job opportunities available, but it is essential to also create an environment where people can develop their cultural values — this would help people more. We can witness this lack of cultural values in society today.

When we hear the word "vazhipādu" ("offering" in Malayalam), the first thing that comes to our mind is the payasam (sweet pudding) offered as naivēdyam to the Lord. Some may ask, "When the poor are hungry, why does the Lord need sweet milk pudding?" Have we ever seen any God eating payasam? It is we ourselves who eat it. What has been offered as naivēdyam to the Lord is later shared among the devotees. Then everyone, including the poor and small children, gets a share of the payasam. When they get an opportunity to eat payasam, the joy that fills their hearts is God's blessed offering, God's prasād, for us. Even though we love payasam, when we share it with others instead of eating it ourselves, our hearts become expansive. Real happiness blossoms in generous hearts. This is the blessing we receive from God through our offerings.

All our actions are to receive God's grace. Thus, it is important to surrender everything to God before beginning any task. The farmer will pray before sowing his seeds. Only then will he sow them. This is because human effort has its limitations. For an action to become complete and to get the desired result, we need God's blessing. The seeds have been sown, and the rice stalks have grown and are now ripe for harvesting. But if there is a flood when the paddy is reaped, the entire harvest will be destroyed. Whatever our actions may be, they attain completion only through grace. Therefore, our ancestors imparted to us the saṁskāra of offering everything first to the Lord before accepting it. Even when we eat, we must offer the first handful to the Lord. This is the attitude of dedication, of surrender, and of sharing. Through this attitude, we bring into practice the awareness that life is not just for myself — it is to share with others. It is also an act by which we offer to the Lord what our mind is attached to.

Let us see what our mind is attached to now. Ninety percent of the time, it is attached to wealth. When wealth and property are being divided, if we receive ten coconut trees less as our share, we will not hesitate to take our own mother to court. When a boy marries a girl, the boy's family will not only check the lineage of the girl's family but also how wealthy they are. We can count on our fingers those who do not do so. So, our minds are attached to wealth. It is not an easy task to free the mind from these attachments. The simplest way is to offer our minds to God. When we offer our mind to God, it becomes pure. We offer our favorite things to God as a token of offering our minds.

Some people say that Lord Kṛishṇa loves milk payasam. In reality, Kṛishṇa is sweet in himself — he is the sweetness of love. But we love payasam the most. When we offer it often to God, we think that God loves milk payasam. In reality, it is an act by which we offer what we love to God. In the true sense, God is love. He delights in our heart's payasam — the payasam of love.

Once, a devotee bought and kept lots of apples, grapes, and delicious eatables inside the pūjā room. Then he says to the Lord, "O Lord! Look at the variety of things that I have bought for you — apples, grapes, delicious snacks — are you content?"

At once, he hears a voice from the heavens. "No, none of this can make me content!"

"O Lord! Please tell me what makes you content. I shall buy it for you."

"There is a flower named mānasa-puṣhpa, the heart flower. I am very fond of that."

"Where will I get it?"

"At the nearest house!"

The devotee immediately went to the neighbor's home, asking for the heart flower. But the neighbors knew nothing about such a flower. He went to every home in the village in search of the flower. Everywhere he received the same answer, "We have never seen or heard of such a flower."

Exhausted, the devotee came and prostrated in front of the Lord and said, "O Lord! Please forgive me. I searched all over the village, but I couldn't find the mānasa-puṣhpa you wanted. I have only my heart to offer you."

"Yes, this is the flower I had asked for: the mānasa-puṣhpa, the flower of your heart. All that you offered me grew through my power. Without my power, you would not be able to even raise your arm. Everything in this world is my creation. But you have created something of your own — the sense of "I." This is what you need to offer me. Your innocent heart is the flower that I like above anything else." This was the Lord's reply.

When hearing this story, you may wonder what is the need to offer flowers to the Lord. This practice is not just a ritual; it also has practical value. Many people grow flowers specifically for this purpose. This becomes a livelihood for them. Some people are employed to pluck those flowers and for others it provides employment opportunities as flower sellers and exporters. When we buy flowers and offer them to the Lord, we feel fulfilled and many people can earn their livelihood from these flowers that bloom today and wither tomorrow. Additionally, those plants which are a part of nature will be protected. We should consider the practical aspects of things. We may feel that garlands made of ribbons and cloth are better than flower garlands. Those garlands are also good as they too provide employment opportunities to many people, but they do not perish in a day. Only a real flower will wither and fall the very next day. Offering flowers to the Lord is a way to make the best use of flowers.

When we gain a fundamental understanding of the real essence of īśhvara (īśhvara tattva) and start loving God, divine qualities will also grow within us. Amma remembers the old days. When the people of this village were about to start their pilgrimage to Sabarimala[10], rice gruel and lentils were cooked and served to everyone coming to see them off. When the irumuḍikkeṭṭu, a cloth bundle divided into two sections – one section containing the sacred offering to the Lord and the other containing food provisions for the journey – was placed on their head (the traditional way to carry it on pilgrimage), they would also give

[10] A famous temple in Kerala dedicated to Lord Ayyappa.

a fistful of coins to the small children who had come to see them leave. Whenever we provide enough food to the hungry to fill their stomachs and give children money to buy sweets, whenever we make someone happy, we are rewarded with contentment. The compassion we show to others comes back to us as God's grace.

When we offer money in temples, it symbolizes our love for God. It is not a bribe. Give something that you love to the person you love – it is the face of love. Love becomes compassion when it is acted upon. We love God. But when we offer something for God's sake, it becomes an act of compassion towards the world. God's grace will flow only to those who give.

Likewise, those who sincerely love God will abandon bad habits. They will not do anything that God would disapprove of. If they do something wrong, they will try very hard not to repeat it. They will save the money they used to fritter away on bad habits and use it to serve the poor. Real worship of God is the compassion we show towards the poor. We will reduce our luxuries. The money we save will be used to serve people in need. We will develop the habit of taking only what is necessary. We will abandon the desire to acquire excessive wealth. We abandon the thought of becoming rich even by grabbing what belongs to another. In this way, it becomes possible to maintain harmony in society.

31

Question: The idols in temples are adorned with costly ornaments. Aren't such expensive adornments against devotion and spirituality?

Amma: We are naturally drawn to beauty; we like and appreciate anything beautiful. This is why we wear ornaments and colorful clothes. But this attraction towards external objects binds us and strengthens our identification with the physical body. However, if we channel our attraction to beauty towards God, it will uplift us. When we adorn God with beautiful objects, we relish God's beauty. The mind becomes singularly focused on God. In reality, God is the epitome and essence of beauty, even without any of these adornments. But at this point, we are capable of enjoying beauty only through an upādhi – a conduit or instrument. Therefore, using the power of our imagination, we decorate the form of God most beautifully.

Long ago, we were ruled by kings. A king has lordship over his kingdom, whereas God is the lord of this entire universe. People saw God with the same attitude and eyes with which they saw their king. They believed that just as the king provided for all his subjects' needs, God provided all that was needed in this world. They visualized God as the king of kings. They adorned the idols of God with regal ornaments and found joy in appreciating their beauty.

Just as a golden pot does not require a golden dot to enhance its beauty, God does not need any particular adornment. He is the beauty in beauty, verily the personification of beauty. But it refreshes the mind when we adorn the idol and see the beautiful form before our eyes. A positive atmosphere is created. Such adornments help to enhance the mood of devotion in the human mind. The devotee becomes wholly absorbed in God's beauty, forgetting everything else.

Until one attains the state of a jīvanmukta, we will seek beauty in external objects, search for beauty everywhere, and desire to be lovelier or more handsome than anyone else. God is the perfection of beauty, so what is wrong with desiring to see God as the most beautiful? The devotee knows that God is the all-pervading, pure consciousness; he is everywhere, both inside and outside. Still, the devotee has a deep longing to see the Lord's divine, beautiful form with their own eyes and to delight in his beauty.

adharam madhuram vadanam madhuram
nayanam madhuram hasitam madhuram
hṛidayam madhuram gamanam madhuram
madhurādhipatēr-akhilam madhuram

His lips are sweet, His face is sweet,
His eyes are sweet, His smile is sweet,
His heart is sweet, His gait is sweet.
Everything is sweet about the lord of sweetness.

(*Madhurāṣhṭakam*, Verse 1)

Thus, devotees find beauty in everything about the Lord. They try to absorb that beauty through all their organs of perception. The five sense-organs are entirely absorbed in the Lord when they see his divine form through their eyes, listen to his song through their ears, partake of his food offering (naivēdyam) with their tongue, touch the cool sandal paste used to adorn him, and inhale the fragrance of the Lord.

He is complete and perfect, whether in the form of a beggar or a king. We adorn him according to our imagination for our own delight. The Lord cannot be confined within our imagination. God is everything; he lacks nothing. Whether we adorn him or not, it does not make him any different.

Amma remembers the story of Śhrī Rāma. It was decided to perform Śhrī Rāma's coronation, and preparations were underway. But the very next moment, when he was asked to go to the forest, he left with complete composure, without any change in his demeanor. If he wanted to, he could have reigned as king. The entire populace was with him. But still, he did not turn back. He did not retract his decision because he was not attached to anything. When we worship the Lord, it is this dispassion we should gain. The costly gifts offered by the devotees do not bind the Lord. They are only adornments. Those adornments are there only for his devotees' contentment. Devotees offer various articles to the Lord. Through their actions, it is the devotees themselves who experience joy. They experience not the joy of taking possession of something but the delight of giving. Gradually, devotees will start to understand that God resides not only in the temple, he dwells in every living being. The attitude to serve everyone, seeing them as God, will grow in them. Temple worship is the beginning of this.

The gold and silver offered as adornments to the Lord do not belong to any individual. It is the wealth of the community of devotees. Don't we buy and keep gold ornaments in our homes? They belong exclusively to us. But temple wealth belongs to the Lord, to the community of devotees. It is they who should decide how to utilize it.

32

Question: What is the principle behind idol worship?

Amma: In reality, Hindus do not worship idols. Instead, through the idol, they worship the omnipresent supreme consciousness. When the son sees his father's portrait, he will not remember the painter who drew it. He remembers his father. When the lover sees the pen or handkerchief his beloved gave him, he remembers his beloved, not the object. He will not be ready to exchange it for anything! The pen his beloved gave him is not a mere pen. The handkerchief his beloved gave him is not a mere handkerchief. In them, he sees his beloved. If a regular young man can have such a bhāva (sentiment), think of the value that a devotee gives to the idol that awakens the remembrance of the God of all beings. For the devotee, the idol is not a mere stone sculpture – it is the embodiment of pure consciousness.

Some may say marriage is only about tying a thread with a tāli (wedding pendant) around the neck. True, it is just a thread being tied around the neck. But we give immense value to the thread and the muhūrta, the auspicious time. It is the muhūrta that lays the foundation for life. The value we give to the thread is not its price value; we give it the value of our entire life. Likewise, the price of the idol is not that of the stone. The value we give to the idol is priceless. Its rank is equal to the Lord of the Universe. A pūjā performed for the idol usually starts with the resolve, "In this, I see and worship God".

It is difficult for regular humans to worship the all-pervading divine consciousness without the aid of an upādhi. The idol is exceedingly helpful in fostering the bhāva of devotion and making the mind one-pointed. Even when we stand before the idol, we close our eyes to pray. Thus, the idol helps us to turn the mind inward and awaken the pure consciousness that dwells within. In Sanātana Dharma, we do not seek God in the external world; we seek inwardly. If we are able to experience God within, then we can see him everywhere.

We should also be aware of the tattva, the principle behind idol worship. God is the foundation of all the ornaments made from gold, be they bangles, earrings, or a finger-ring. Likewise, God is the foundation of everything. We should see oneness in diversity. Whether Śhiva, Viṣhṇu, or Muruga, we should see the oneness of all deities. We should know that all forms are the different aspects of the one God. An actor may take on many roles, but only one person is behind all the roles. People have different saṁskāras (mental predispositions). Hence, God has accepted many forms so that they may be able to worship him in the form and bhāva (mood, attitude) they love. Only Sanātana Dharma grants this freedom to humanity.

If we need to see our face clearly in a mirror, we need to wipe away all the dust and dirt encrusted on the mirror's surface. Likewise, we can get the vision of God only if we clean our mind of all its accumulated impurities. Our ancestors have prescribed worship of the vigraha (idol, physical representation or manifestation of a deity) and other traditional observances because they help to cleanse our mental impurities and to make the mind one-pointed.

In reality, God has no inside or outside. God is the all-pervading, pure consciousness present everywhere. Because we have a sense of individuality, a sense of "I," we feel there is an inside and an outside. At present, our mind is extroverted. It is bound by its attachment to many objects. It is not an easy task to make such a mind introverted. For this, we use the upādhi of the vigraha. Through this, we are able to make our minds one-pointed, grow firm in our devotion, and turn the mind inward. The devotee who looks at the idol and prays to it does not consider that God is limited to this vigraha.

33

Question: Is it possible to say when idol worship began?

Amma: It began in satya yuga[11]. In answer to the asura king Hiraṇyakaśhipu's question, his young son Prahlāda replied, "God is present even in this pillar." This can be said to be the first vigraha or idol. From the pillar, God emerged in the form of Narasiṁha, the half-man, half-lion incarnation of Lord Viṣhṇu. The all-pervading God made Prahlāda's words and resolve true by manifesting from the pillar.

Prahlāda's story is famous! Hiraṇyakaśhipu had done great penance to obtain boons from Brahmā that he would conquer the three worlds and achieve immortality. Gratified by the severe penance undertaken by the asura king, Brahmā appeared before him and asked what he wanted. "I should not die at the hands of any being in your creation. I should not die either on land or on water. I should not die on the earth or in the sky. I should not die either inside or outside a room. I should not die during the day or at night. I should not be killed by either man or woman. I should not be killed by the dēvas or asuras, nor by reptiles. I should not be killed by a human or

---

[11] Oldest of the four yugas or ages, which marks the onset of the decline of dharma.

animal. I should not die by any weapon." "So be it!" Brahmā blessed him and disappeared.

While Hiraṇyakaśhipu was away performing his penance, the dēvas (demi-gods) defeated the asuras (demons). Indra, the king of the dēvas, bound Hiraṇyakaśhipu's pregnant wife and took her along with him. On the way Indra met Sage Nārada. Obeying Nārada's advice, Indra allowed the pregnant Kayādhu to stay in the sage's ashram and went on his way back to dēvalōka, his abode. Sage Nārada taught Kayādhu the bhagavad-tattva, the essential knowledge of God. The child within the mother's womb heard every single word.

Hiraṇyakaśhipu returned after ending his severe penance and swiftly defeated the dēvas. He brought his wife, who had stayed at Sage Nārada's ashram, back to the palace. Arrogant and egoistic with the strength of his boons, he conquered the three worlds and made the defeated dēvas his servants. He tormented the sages and devotees of God and destroyed yajñas (sacred fire rituals). He ordered that from now onwards, no one should utter the names of God; they should only chant "ōm hiraṇyāya namaḥ – I bow down to Hiraṇyakaśhipu!"

In due time, Kayādhu delivered a baby boy. The infant was named Prahlāda. With Nārada's words imprinted in his mind, he grew up as a devotee of Lord Viṣhṇu. When it was time for his education, his father sent him to a gurukula. After a while, he became impatient to know the extent of his son's knowledge. He summoned Prahlāda to the palace and asked him, "What have you learned?" Prahlāda replied,

śhravaṇaṁ kīrtanaṁ viṣhṇōḥ
smaraṇaṁ pāda-sēvanam
archanaṁ vandanaṁ dāsyaṁ
sakhyam ātma-nivēdanam

śhravaṇam — hearing; *kīrtanam* — chanting;
viṣhṇōḥ — of Lord Viṣhṇu (not anyone else);
smaraṇam — remembering;
pāda-sēvanam — serving the feet;
archanam — offering worship (with *ṣhoḍaśhopachāra,* the sixteen kinds of paraphernalia);
vandanam — offering prayers;
dāsyam — being his attendant,
sakhyam — being his best friend,
ātmā-nivēdanam — offering oneself; these are the nine ways in which to worship the Lord.

(*Bhāgavatam* 7.5.23)

Hiraṇyakaśhipu became blind with anger on hearing his own son talk about worshiping his enemy Viṣhṇu. He ordered his soldiers to kill the child. They tried in many ways but were unable to kill Prahlāda. The disappointed Hiraṇyakaśhipu sent his son once again to the gurukula with orders to wipe out his devotion to God. However, listening to Prahlāda's teachings, all the other asura children in the gurukula also became devotees of God. Hearing about this, Hiraṇyakaśhipu became furious. "If there is any God other than me in these three worlds, where is this God? Prahlāda answered, "God is present everywhere. He resides both in the pillar and in a speck of rust." Hiraṇyakaśhipu roared in fury, "Aha! Is he dwelling in this pillar?" Prahlāda answered, "Yes, he also dwells within this pillar." Hearing his son's reply, Hiraṇyakaśhipu struck the pillar with all his might. The pillar split apart, and the terrifying form of Narasiṁha, half man and half lion, emerged from it. It was dusk. The Lord sat on the palace steps, placed Hiraṇyakaśhipu on his lap, and with his claws tore open his chest.

The sages have experienced the supreme truth, and truth will come into their words. Prahlāda answered his father, "God also resides in this pillar." This became the truth. God manifested from the pillar. This is why it is said that truth comes and enters the words of the sages. Usually, a new creation comes from the mother's womb. However, the sages' resolve itself becomes a new creation. That is, whatever they say becomes the truth. They know the past, present, and future. Therefore, their words are also for the future generations.

This incident also reveals another principle — the reality of human limitations. God's intelligence transcends that of the most powerful and super intelligent human beings living in this world. Human intelligence is limited, but divine intelligence is unlimited.

Hiraṇyakaśhipu had pondered deeply before asking boons from Brahmā — he should not meet death in any way whatsoever. When he received such a boon, Hiraṇyakaśhipu assumed there was none in the world to challenge him. But he was unable to understand the nature of God. The solution to everything is in God's hands. When the Lord approached Hiraṇyakaśhipu, it was neither day nor night – it was dusk; neither in water nor on earth – he laid the asura on his lap; neither inside nor outside – on the threshold of the palace steps; neither man nor animal – Narasiṁha, the man-lion; not by weapons – he used his claws. Without breaking even a single aspect of Brahmā's boon, the Lord took the form of Narasiṁha and slew the evil and adharmic Hiraṇyakaśhipu.

The Lord transcends human intellect. There is only one way to know him: to offer ourselves totally at his divine feet – complete surrender.

Humans have two kinds of intellect: the egoistic intellect, ahaṅkāra-buddhi, and the wise and discerning intellect, vivēka-buddhi. Vivēka-buddhi is clear, without impurities. It is like a mirror in which God is clearly reflected. Only those who offer their intellect to God will be able to transcend its limitations and go beyond.

Prahlāda exemplifies the most ideal type of devotion. It is difficult to find another person who has such surrender. When we go and pray to God, if we do not receive what we desire, we will blame him and return without any more prayers. Our faith will be lost when we have to undergo hardship. We will blame God. But look at Prahlāda: the soldiers tried to drown him; they threw him into a cauldron of boiling oil; they threw him off a cliff; they threw him into a fire. Thus, they attempted to kill him many times and in many ways.

Yet Prahlāda's devotion did not wane or falter even the tiniest bit. And that faith saved him from all danger. He stood there in the midst of all danger, chanting, "Nārāyaṇa, Nārāyaṇa." Finally, many tried to destroy his faith in God by telling him, "Śhrīhari is a thief. He is not God. There is no such thing as God." Even when they tried to convince him with such words, Prahlāda calmly, with total awareness, continued to chant the name of Nārāyaṇa. But our faith will be lost if someone says something derogatory about another to us.

If sorrow comes to us, our faith will be lost. Our devotion is part-time. We call out to God if we need anything. If not, we will not even remember him. And suppose our desires are not fulfilled? Then we stop believing in God. This is our attitude. Each daunting challenge only strengthened Prahlāda's faith. As the severity of his challenges escalated, so did his surrender to God. He clung tighter to the Lord's feet. Such was the magnitude of his surrender. By virtue of his surrender, Prahlāda became a shining light, illuminating the world with his life. To this day, his story and the depth of his faith continue to illumine the lives of thousands.

Prahlāda's devotion also led to his father Hiraṇyakaśhipu's liberation. To die in God's hands is liberation. It means that identification with the body has been destroyed, and knowledge of the self has been revealed. The body is ephemeral. Hiraṇyakaśhipu was given experiential knowledge that only the self is eternal.

Insignificant and egoistic human beings often become arrogant in their intellect and abilities, leading them to criticize God. God is a reality beyond the human intellect. The sages have advised us to know God through worshiping the vigraha and various spiritual practices.

34

Question: Some people condemn the Hindu religion because of idol worship. Is there any truth to this?

Amma: The worship of vigrahas (physical representations of God) is prevalent in every religion, in one way or another, so one does not know the intention behind their condemnation of the Hindu religion. Idol worship exists in Christianity and Islam. It exists in Buddhism. In the Christian faith, followers kneel and pray before Christ's statue. They do not offer payasam and flowers; instead, they light a candle. They see Christ's flesh in the bread and his blood in the wine and offer it. If Hindus worship God with camphor, Christians worship God with frankincense. Christians see the cross as a symbol of sacrifice. Mecca is seen as sacred in Islam, and so Muslims prostrate and pray in the direction of Mecca. They sit before the Kaaba, reflect on God's qualities, and pray. All these prayers are meant to awaken good qualities within us.

In Malayalam, we learn the letters "ka, kha, ga, gha, ṅa" to read words with compound letters. We learn A, B, C, D to read English words. Likewise, all these forms of worship are meant to make the mind one-pointed towards God and to develop divine qualities in us. Others condemn idol worship because they do not know the principle behind vigraha ārādhanā, adoration of a physical form. We should remove their ignorance. But it is very difficult to awaken those who pretend to be asleep.

35

Question: Shouldn't we worship the sculptor more than the idol he sculpted?

Amma: When we see the flag of a political party, do we revere the person who stitched it? Or the one who wove the cloth? Or the one who spun the thread to weave the cloth? Or the one who cultivated the cotton needed to spin the thread? No one remembers them. Instead, we remember the political party. Likewise, when we see the vigraha or idol, we do not recollect its sculptor; we remember God, the sculptor of this universe. God is the power who gave the sculptor the motivation and the ability to sculpt the vigraha. If we agree that a sculptor is needed to sculpt a vigraha, where is the issue in thinking that this universe may also have a sculptor?

Through adoration of the vigraha, we gain the broadness of mind to honor the sculptor, and to love and revere every living being. When we visualize the God of all beings in the vigraha and pray to him, our minds become pure and uplifted.

We are able to see and worship God in everything. This is the aim of vigraha ārādhanā, worship of a physical representation of God. All symbols that remind humanity of the material world will bind it within its limitations. The vigrahas, the symbols that bring alive the remembrance of God, however, will lead humankind to expansiveness. It gives us the ability to see God in everything.

36

Question: Do those who go to temples understand the fundamental principles behind temple worship?

Amma: The number of people going to temples has increased, but it is doubtful whether the level of our saṁskāra (culture) is growing in proportion. Mechanisms to adequately explain our saṁskāra can be said to be almost nil in our temples. Therefore, people see temples only as instruments to achieve their desires. Nowadays, only desires come to the forefront when people go to temples and close their eyes. It is not wrong to have desires. But we cannot experience peace of mind when our mind is overflowing with desires. Many people go to temples because they fear that if they do not pray to God, dangers will befall them. God protects us in every way. When we truly worship God, we gain total freedom from fear.

Nowadays, temple worship has become a mere imitation. People are ignorant of its fundamental principles. The son went to the temple along with his father. The father circumambulated the temple and the son followed. When the son became a father, he took his own son to the temple and repeated whatever was done before. But he wouldn't know the reasons why he observes these rituals. There are no channels in the temple to explain and make him understand the reasons why.

A man used to perform pūjā daily in his family temple. One day, after he had prepared everything for the pūjā, the family cat came in and lapped up the milk kept for offering to the Lord as naivēdyam. The next day, after he had prepared all the items for the pūjā, he caught the cat and kept it under a basket. He let it free only after the pūjā ended. It is true that God also dwells in the cat. But in saguṇa ārādhanā, i.e. worship of the deity with form, external cleanliness is essential. External purity leads us to internal purity. The man made it a habit to catch the cat and keep it under the basket before every pūjā. After some time, the man died, and his son started performing the pūjā daily. He also continued the habit of enclosing the cat under the basket. One day, when the son searched for the cat before starting the pūjā, he couldn't find it anywhere. He learned that the cat had died. Without waiting for even a moment, he brought the next-door neighbor's cat over and trapped it under the basket. Only then did he start the pūjā.

The son had never asked why his father had kept the cat underneath the basket. He followed his father's example, and it never occurred to him to ask why. Many of us observe our traditions this way. We do not try to understand their meaning, gain knowledge about the principles they are founded on. We imitate our elders. This is not how it should be. Whatever the religion, we should grasp the tattva, the essential principles, behind the traditions and rituals. When we understand the true meaning of our traditions and customs, anāchāras or bad customs will not prevail; or if they do, we will be able to disown them.

It is not enough to go to the temple every day and have the darśhan (vision) of the deity. We must also make time daily to meditate on God and try to chant as many mantras as possible. Once we enter the temple, we should try to center our mind on God and keep it there. We should circumambulate silently, with our mind chanting the mantra. When we stand in front of the shrine and have the deity's darśhan, we should close our eyes, see the vigraha within our hearts and meditate upon it.

Arrangements should be made in temples to make people understand the meaning of spirituality and the foundational knowledge behind the traditions and ritual observances. Temples should become centers which make man's heart rich in their saṁskāra (culture). Only then can we regain our glorious heritage.

37

Question: What is genuine devotion?

Amma: Some people believe that devotion means worshiping different gods in temples. Others dismiss devotion because they too think devotion is limited to just temple worship. But no one can criticize devotion if they also understand īśhvara-tattva, the foundational knowledge of the personal God, who is pure and infinite. Genuine devotion is desireless self-surrender with the knowledge that it is the one God who manifests as all the names and forms and in all beings – it is the one God who shines through all forms of divinity.

Both the jñāni (a self-realized person) who meditates on the fact that, "I am not the body, mind, or intellect, neither do I have merit or demerit; I am the ātman," and the devotee who prays, "All is You, I am nothing," are in reality discerning between the eternal and the transitory (conducting nitya-anitya vivēka). Real prayer is such discernment. A genuine devotee prays with the attitude, 'Only God is eternal; everything else is transitory.' Prayer awakens positive vibrations in our minds. It will usher good thoughts into our minds as we perform each action. Like digging a well to get water, we awaken our inner strength through prayer.

It is very difficult to attain dedication (niṣṭha) if knowledge (jñāna) is lacking devotion (bhakti). When we whitewash a wall, we need to add some glue for the lime powder to stick properly. Our mind is like this lime powder. We can reach God only if the glue of love is present. We cannot construct a building with just bricks and metal. We need to add cement. Without the cement of love, it is not possible to build the steps to reach God.

Anyone who suffers from indigestion or other diseases may have dietary restrictions. But everyone can eat gruel made from small pieces of broken rice. It is easily digestible. Likewise, the path of devotion is suitable for everyone. An upādhi, an instrument, is needed to make the mind one-pointed towards God. Devotion is that instrument. Devotion is the enthusiasm and inspiration to realize the goal. Just as we use surgical spirit to clean a wound, devotion is the spirit that cleanses the mind.

There is a saying, "We can be born in a temple, but we should not die there." In the eyes of a devotee, God resides in all beings, sentient and insentient. God's power is not limited to an idol or a temple. God is not a power that resides beyond the sky. God is the pure consciousness that pervades the entire universe. Our devotion should not confine itself to worshiping the vigraha; it should grow to a state where we can perceive God in everything.

When we climb up on the terrace of a bungalow and look down, we see that the steps we climbed, the rooms below, and the terrace are all constructed of the same sand, cement, and metal rods. Likewise, a devotee who travels forward through the path of prayer, ritualistic worship, chanting the divine names, etc., will finally realize that, "All is God; there is nothing but God."

When our ancestors woke up in the morning, they would touch the ground with reverence and fold their palms in prayer before stepping on it. The earth was not merely mud for them. It was the Goddess. It was their mother. During the rainy season, even before stepping over small rivulets, they would bend down and touch the water with reverence. They thought, "Even this is God, so how can we step on God and cross over?" In the eyes of a genuine devotee, rivers, mountains, trees, plants, and flowers are all God. Long ago, before cutting down a tree, an auspicious day would be chosen, and prayers would be offered to seek forgiveness from the tree and to request permission to cut it down. The tree would be felled only after ritualisitic worship was offered to it. They saw the divine consciousness in the tree. The children who grew up observing all this also learned to see God in everything.

Amma remembers a story: Once, a robber fatally wounded a mahātmā. Hearing about this, the mahātmā's disciples went in search of their guru and saw him lying on the roadside covered in blood. The disciples carried the Guru to the ashram. They cared for him with love and put medicine on his wounds. When they saw that their master was nearing death, a disciple gently poured the sacred water of the Ganga into his mouth and asked him, "O Master! Do you recognize me?" "Child, the same hands that wounded me are now pouring the water of the Ganga into my mouth." He saw the same God in friend, enemy, and all beings, both sentient and insentient. This is the attitude we should gain through devotion.

The jñāni who perceives the ātman in everything, realizes that there is nothing separate from himself in this world. In contrast, the devotee sees only his dearest God in everything. In their perfection, both bhakti (devotion) and jñāna (knowledge) are the same. The difference is only in external attitudes.

38

Question: Amma, you say that we should have śhraddhā, bhakti, and viśhvāsa. What is meant by these?

Amma: Sanātana Dharma teaches us śhraddhā — knowledge and awareness; bhakti — devotion; and viśhvāsa — trust. It does not ask you to believe or trust in anything unquestioningly. When we use a machine we should know how to operate it, otherwise it will break down. Jñāna is true knowledge about something. When actions are performed with such true knowledge and awareness, it becomes śhraddhā.

Once, a man started pouring water into a water tank to fill it. He kept pouring until evening, but still, the tank wasn't full. Upon discovering that his hard work was not yielding the expected outcome, he began investigating. Then he discovered why — one of the openings at the bottom of the tank had not been closed. Whatever the quantity of water poured into the tank, unless that opening is closed, it will have no effect — here, this knowledge is jñāna. We will get the expected result only if our actions are performed with awareness and true knowledge, i.e. with śhraddhā.

Five people were entrusted with the task of farming. One came and dug the holes, another added the fertilizers, and yet another watered each hole. Then another came and closed the holes. Many days passed, but no seedlings came up. Upon inquiry, they discovered that the fifth person who was responsible for placing the seeds in each hole had failed to do so. Actions performed without śhraddhā can be compared to this. They will not give the expected result.

Each action we perform in life should bring us closer to God. We should perform our actions without the sense of doership or desire. We should be aware that God's grace and power are allowing us to perform any task. This is true knowledge or jñāna, in action. Actions performed with this jñāna and śhraddhā become karma yōga — actions that unite us with the divine. When we are completely engrossed in our work, with perfect śhraddhā, we forget ourselves; the mind becomes one-pointed, and we experience joy. This is the point where bhakti is born.

Thus, our actions bear the perfect fruits when we act with śhraddhā and bhakti. When we receive the benefits, the fruits of our actions, our viśhvāsa — our faith — becomes firm. Such a faith is unshakeable. None can weaken it. Śhraddhā, bhakti, viśhvāsa — actions performed with śhraddhā nurture bhakti, and this leads to viśhvāsa. Most of the scriptural texts in Sanātana Dharma are in the form of dialogues. They are answers to the disciple's doubts. The disciple is free to question the Guru until his doubts are completely cleared. In this way, śhraddhā (faith in God, Guru, and scriptures gained from removal of doubts from the mind) grows in the disciple. Once we gain śhraddhā, everything else will be easy.

39

Question: It is said that devotion should be selfless. If so, is it wrong to pray to God to remove our sorrows?

Amma: If our hearts are heavy with sorrow, there is nothing wrong with unburdening them to God. We can share our hearts with God and place our burdens before him. But our prayers should be for devotion. Only then can anything come to perfect fruition. Do not think that God will know only if you tell him everything.

You must open up and disclose everything to a lawyer and a doctor. Only then can the lawyer argue your case properly or the doctor treat your disease correctly. But even though you do not say anything to God, he will know everything. Because he is all-knowing. He is the in-dweller of our hearts. We should pray to be able to love God. When our prayer becomes only for God, then even without asking, he will fulfill our material needs. We must pray to be one with him. Then his grace will naturally flow towards us; we will be filled with divine qualities.

When we pray to God, we must know the tattva or underlying truth — that God is the omniscient and omnipresent consciousness. Instead of believing that there are different Gods, we should realize that they are different forms of the one God. We should worship God with love. He knows our mind's desires. Even so, it is not wrong to open our hearts before him. However, we should understand that this is only the initial phase. Gradually, we should learn to worship God without any desire. If devotion is for the sake of devotion, we will gain everything from it. We will have material gain and spiritual progress. We can realize God only through innocent, loving devotion.

40

Question: How long do we have to pray every day to gain the experience of God?

Amma: Worshiping God is part-time for many people. Devotion shouldn't be part-time. We need full-time devotion. Praying to fulfill a desire is part-time devotion. We need devotion for the sake of devotion. Our desire should only be to love God. We should pray for this. We should have constant remembrance of God. We should be able to perceive him in everything. It is he who gives us the strength to pray. Without his strength, we wouldn't even be able to lift our hands. We wouldn't even be able to move a single finger. This constant awareness that God is the power behind all my actions is full-time devotion. With this, we become free of the sense of "I," which arises from our identification with the body, mind, and intellect. We are able to become one with the all-pervasive divine consciousness.

Haven't you heard the story of Kālīdāsa? Once, Kālīdāsa went inside the temple's inner shrine and closed the doors. Dēvī came and knocked on the doors. The doors remained closed. Dēvī asked, "Who is inside?" The answer came from behind the closed doors as a counter question, "Who is outside?" Finally, Dēvī replied, "Kālī is outside," and from inside, the answer came, "Dāsa — your servant — is inside." Even though he was asked many times to reveal his identity, he did not even give his name. Only when he heard that "Kālī is outside" did the answer come: "Dāsa — your servant — is inside." In that very moment, Kālīdāsa received the complete and perfect experience of divinity. When the "I" is lost, only "You" remains. We must lose our small identity, the sense of "I." Everything is "You" — we must be aware that it is God who makes us perform every action. This is true devotion. Through this, we will receive everything; there is nothing more for us to gain.

It is God who gives sight to our eyes. So, he doesn't need the light from the ten-rupee wick we light in front of him. God has nothing to gain from us. It is we who gain by depending on God. We make an offering to God as a symbol of our surrender. Thus, the attitude of surrender grows in us. Not only that, smoke from the oil or ghee lamp that we light in front of God's image purifies the atmosphere. We should not think that we can make an offering and bribe God to gain our desires.

Even top-quality seeds will not germinate if kept in the hand. We must be willing to bury them in the earth. The fruits will come only when we surrender. Likewise, we should let go of the attitude of "mine" and of getting "my desires" fulfilled. We should develop the attitude that, "Everything is Yours" and, "Let Your will be done." Devotion attains perfection only when this attitude of surrender develops in us. Then prayer will not be said at a specific time. God's remembrance will be there at all times.

41

Question: Some people criticize devotion, faith in God, and spirituality, as superstitions and weaknesses of the mind that are used as instruments for exploitation. Can we say that such labeling is unfounded?

Amma: Criticism is valuable when it awakens a spirit of genuine enquiry within us. If it doesn't, it becomes merely blind judgment.

Devotion is a practical science, a practical way of life, and a great help in bringing harmony to individuals and to society. When we think of its practical benefits, we cannot say that devotion is a weakness of the mind. When faced with difficulties and sorrows, many go to the prayer room, share their grief with their iṣhṭa-dēvatā, their cherished deity's form, and pray. This is a practical method to unburden the mind. For the believer, it gives consolation, hope, and confidence in oneself.

A balloon will burst if too much air is pumped into it. Likewise, if the mind is filled with problems and conflicts, we lose the balance and harmony of life itself. Devotion is the practical means to lay down the heavy burdens of the mind, and to uplift the weary mind. Our problems cease when our inner conflicts cease. We lament about various issues bothering us to others. But the result can be compared to a small rat snake trying to swallow a giant frog. Instead of the expected relief, the problems and difficulties may escalate. But if we depend on God with faith and trust, our minds will definitely become peaceful. Crying and shedding tears out of devotion is not a weakness. When the candle melts, its flame becomes brighter. Likewise, when we pray to God, we amass the strength to face life's problems.

Another benefit of devotion is the improvement and refinement of our nature and character. We will obey whatever the person we love most asks us to do. When a girl tells the man who loves her, "If you love me, you should stop smoking cigarettes." If the man loves her sincerely, he will give up the bad habit. This is love. Instead, if he has second thoughts on obeying her, there is no love there. There is no duality in love. Many have stopped their bad habits because their loved ones have asked them to do so. "She doesn't like it when I drink. So I stopped." We may ask, "Isn't this a weakness?" If you look at its benefits, it is definitely not a weakness. On the contrary, it is strength. We cannot relish love when logic or rational thinking enters into it. There is only love in love; there is no place for logic.

Devotion and faith become the reason for us to do good deeds and refrain from doing wrong actions. Traffic rules reduce accidents. Likewise, devotion and spirituality are the practical means to sustain harmony in society. It also nourishes the awareness of dharma and the right values in humanity.

All paths of devotion emphasize an individual's responsibility towards society. Devotion to God and compassion towards fellow beings are like two sides of the same coin. If one is present, the other will also be present. The compassion we show towards the poor is God's real worship. Devotion inspires us to serve people experiencing poverty with our excess wealth rather than to accumulate it for ourselves. Giving to the poor in the neighborhood is integral to most ceremonies founded on devotion.

When starting the pilgrimage to Sabarimala, as we lift the bundled offering onto our heads, it is customary to take fistfuls of coins and give them to children. After worship rituals like pūjās and hōmas conclude, it is customary to feed the poor and to perform many acts of charity. Thus, devotion helps to deepen awareness of our responsibility to society and compassion for all living beings. Likewise, *sarpa pūjā* (snake worship) and *kāvu tīndātirikkaḷ* (not entering sacred groves)[12] were all traditions that protected the environment.

---

[12] *Kāvu tīndātirikkaḷ* refers to the traditional practice in Kerala of not entering or disturbing kāvu – sacred groves that are left untouched to serve as sanctuaries

We do not need intellectual gymnastics; we need practical benefits. We tell children that if they lie, it will harm their eyes. This is not true, but this harmless lie helps to guide children down the right path. Even if we are unable to explain some of the traditions associated with devotion logically, it benefits people in many ways. It is a way to connect with and uplift people at their level.

Some may exploit devotion and spirituality. Fake coins are minted only because the original has great value. Is there any meaning in banning all books because a few describe different ways to steal?

Love and faith are the greatest treasures humanity has received. Without them, life would be as lifeless as a corpse wearing makeup. I am not saying that we do not need logic and intellect. They have their own place. Both the scissors that snip cloth into pieces and the needle that stitches them together have their own place. The problem is not whether God exists or not; it is whether

---

for snakes and other wildlife. These groves are considered holy and off-limits to human activity, reflecting a deep respect for nature and contributing to environmental conservation.

humanity experiences sorrow. We should think of practical ways to find solutions. Devotion is the way by which the solution to sorrow is found within oneself. Its relevance and practical benefits are ever-lasting.

Some say, "Is it possible to see God with our eyes? I will not believe what I cannot see." Man is limited in every way. His sight and hearing are in themselves limited. But such people do not ponder this fact. Let me ask something: We cannot see the current in the wire. But can we say that there is no current in the wires? If we touch a live wire, we will suffer an electric shock. That is an experience.

We let free a bird. It flew up into the vast sky and disappeared from our sight. But can we say the bird does not exist because we cannot see it? Where is the logic in saying that I will only believe what I can see within the purview of my eyesight?

The judge does not consider the fact that a thousand people did not see a murder being committed; he takes as evidence the words of the one person who saw the act of murder. Likewise, even if many say that there is no God, proof exists as the words of the ancient sages who have experienced God.

We say that the seed contains the tree. If we examine it or bite into it, we will not be able to see the tree. But plant the seed; make an effort. Then we will see the tiny sapling emerging from the seed. It is not enough to talk. We must make an effort. Then we will experience the truth of it.

Even if a scientist has a purely materialistic viewpoint, he places trust in his experiments. Many of his experiments may fail, yet he will not stop his efforts. He continues his research, believing he will succeed in his next experiment. How many years does it take to become a doctor or an engineer? No one complains that they cannot wait for so many years. They graduate from medical school or earn an engineering degree only after studying with dedication for all those years.

God is not someone we can see with our eyes. He is the primal cause. What answer can we give to the question of whether the mango or the mango seed came first? The mango seed is needed for the mango tree to germinate, and the mango tree has to grow for us to get a mango seed. So, both of them need another cause, another reason for being. This is God, the original cause of everything. He is the creator of all. God is everything. The way to know God is to cultivate divine qualities within us and to surrender our ego to him. Then godliness — divinity — will become our experience.

42

Question: Some people cry and pray. Isn't this a weakness? Doesn't energy get dissipated through this?

Amma: Crying when praying to God is not a weakness. Crying for ordinary things is like burning firewood for no reason. But crying while praying to God is like cooking delicious sweet pudding with the firewood we burn. We receive sweetness from it. The brightness of a candle increases as it keeps melting. At times, thinking and crying over worldly matters may reduce the heart's burden. But we should not keep crying over the past and what may happen in the future. If we keep crying over whether our child will study and pass the exams, over the injustice we think someone did to us, or over what others will say — it will only pave the way for depression and other illnesses.

This is a weakness. But, when we open our heart and pray to God, our mind is at peace.

Crying for God nurtures good qualities in us. Crying and praying help keep the mind that would otherwise run after the world's objects in one place. The mind becomes focused and one-pointed. So, we are not dissipating our energy; we are amassing it. It is a shortcut to bring the mind into our own hands. Even though God dwells within us, our minds have not yet turned inward towards God. Crying and praying are a way to keep the mind on God, just like children get their mother's attention by their tears. If a child says he is hungry, the mother may turn and look at him. But if the child cries, the mother will run to him, pick him up, and feed him milk. Crying while we pray is an excellent way to bring the mind under our control. Therefore, it is not a weakness.

On the path of self-inquiry, it is with the mind that we negate and say: "I am not the body, mind, or intellect, I have neither merit nor demerit. It is with the mind that we affirm: I am the ātman." For those who have not learned meditation, yōga, or the scriptural texts, crying and prayer are a simple means for bringing the mind under our control. It is also a kind of negation when we open our heart, lay down our sorrows to God, and pray with tears to know his real nature.

43

Question: Isn't it a sign of weakness to pray out loud?

Amma: Some read silently, while others like to read out loud. Only then will their mind stay on the topic. Many sing out loud and enjoy themselves, whereas many others calmly hum their songs. Each person accepts what they like. It is not right to say that what some people do is a weakness. It is their way.

Even though God is within, our mind is not. Even if a pot is kept in front of us, if our mind is not with the pot, we will not see it. When someone speaks, if our mind is not with the speaker, we will not hear him. Likewise, God resides within us, but as our mind has not turned inward, we cannot know Him.

Usually, our mind is caught up in many things. We should bring the mind back from them and center it on God. When we do so, love, compassion, equal vision, and other divine qualities are awakened within us. We must fill ourselves, both inside and outside, with these qualities so that they benefit others. This is what happens through prayer also.

A son came and told Amma that he didn't like to pray. "Where is the need for all this?" Amma replied, "Son, let me ask you something. If you had a lover, would you dislike talking to her? You would enjoy it. Similar is prayer for a devotee. The Lord is everything to the devotee." Amma continued to ask him, "If someone came and told you, 'I do not like you talking to your lover,' how would you respond? Would you give any value to his words? This is how we feel when you come to us now and tell us about your opinions on prayer. Love for God is not ordinary love. It is pure."

Devotion is not like the attachment between a lover and his beloved. In the material realm, the boy desires the girl's love. The girl longs for the boy to love her. They enjoy each other's love. But their love will never be perfect because each one is a beggar. But the devotee's prayer to the Lord is very different. Devotees pray to the Lord to nourish the divine qualities within and to give them a heart big enough to love everyone as if they were God. This is why the devotee shares his heart's sentiments with the Lord. He does not depend on anyone else but the indwelling God to share his heart. The devotee not only nourishes divine qualities within, but he also uses them for the welfare of others.

An ordinary human shares his heart with many others, but he also yearns for love from others in return. But the devotee prays, "Bless me so that I may become like You. Give me the strength to love everyone. Give me the strength to be patient and forgiving."

Bhajans (devotional songs) evoke inner bliss in the devotee. Worldly people gain it from external objects. No danger arises from inner bliss. Once we know how to revel in ourselves, we do not seek bliss in the outer world. Will we search for tasty food outside if we get it at home? When we pray, we find a resting place within ourselves. This path is not like that of a candle that has to be lit by someone else. It is self-effulgent. On this path, we find the light within ourselves.

Prayer gives repose to the mind. We can also gain relaxation from the external world, but it does not last. On the material plane, contentment is gained when our cravings are satiated. In worldly relationships, we feel sad if someone we love doesn't talk to us, and they feel sad if we don't talk to them. When neither one is getting satisfaction from the relationship, they will seek out new relationships. This cycle continues while both of them suffer.

When we go to someone to share our sorrows, they also have only their own sorrows to talk about. Those who go seeking relief come back with double the burden of sorrow. Like the spider that dies in the very web that it weaves, this is what binds us. This state is like that of a very small rat snake trying to swallow a very big frog.

The only way to free ourselves is by becoming a witness to everything. Prayer also aims for this state. Two women were neighbors. One woman's husband died. The woman wailed in grief. The other woman consoled her, "Is there anyone who is deathless? If not today, then tomorrow; it can happen to anyone. Even if the lightbulb fuses, the current is not destroyed. Likewise, only the body has ended; the ātman is indestructible." She consoled the widow with such words. After a few days, the son of the other woman died. The woman beat her chest in agony and wailed in sorrow. Then the widow came and approached her friend who was crying out loud. "When my husband died, you were the one who came to me and consoled me. Please remember the words you told me then." Whatever she said, the other woman couldn't stop her tears. She was wholly identified with her sorrow. But a few days earlier when she had stood aside and seen her friend's sorrow with the attitude of a witness, she was able to console her. She could impart strength to her.

The more we identify with a situation, the more our sorrow increases. But when we are able to stand aside and watch each situation in a witness state, our strength is augmented. We read about an air crash in the newspaper. If our own children or relatives had been on the ill-fated aircraft, we would be overcome with sorrow and unable to read the lines about it in the paper. But if no near and dear ones were involved in the crash, we would finish reading about it and start scanning the paper for other news items. When love for God arises in us, we can see the situations in our life with the attitude of a witness because our mind is anchored to God.

We may experience sorrow from our worldly attachments. If one person's love seems to be lacking, the other may get angry and resentful.

This bond has desire at its forefront. There is desire, expectation, and a sense of entitlement in such relationships. Praying to God also releases us from such attachments. When we pray to God and sing God's songs, we do not expect anything in return. (And still, we get everything.)

Real prayer is when we say, "Please give us Your qualities and the strength to do selfless service." This does not mean we cannot share our sorrows with the Lord. We can lay down all our sorrows in front of him. We can share all our troubles with him and reduce the burden of our hearts. But we should not simply ask, "Give me this... give me that." Our hearts should become greedy to receive the Lord's qualities of love, compassion, peace, etc. Chant the Lord's name, perform good actions, and pray for his grace; he will give us all we need. There is no need to ask for anything.

In school, children are given impositions[13]. When a forgotten lesson is repeated ten times, it is never forgotten again. It becomes imprinted in your awareness. Likewise, through prayer,

[13] When children forget a lesson or have made too many mistakes, they are sometimes asked to write down the same sentence a set number of times.

when we repeatedly make an effort to constantly remember the divine qualities of God, they become a part of our nature, always present in our awareness. A devotee who awakens these qualities within himself is not bound by them and finally reaches a state that transcends all guṇas or qualities (guṇātīta); they become completely detached, a witness to everything. By nouṛiṣhing the divine qualities within, the devotee becomes capable of forgetting himself in the love and service of others. Their individuality ceases to exist. This is the state of guṇātīta.

44

Question: Are there any benefits arising from singing devotional songs, praying, and chanting the Lord's names?

Amma: Many people sing romantic songs. What would the reply be if we asked them, "Where is the benefit in singing such songs? Instead, why don't you perform actions?" The benefits are known to those who have experienced them. People listen to ordinary songs and enjoy them. Likewise, when devotees listen to devotional songs, they are able to dissolve in them and forget themselves. Ordinary songs evoke the feelings of sensual passions and worldly attachments. Whereas when we sing devotional songs and say prayers, the minds of the singer and listener become relaxed and at peace and dissolve in the Lord's form.

Disco songs and other songs of the same kind awaken the vibrations of heavy emotions. When we hear romantic songs, it awakens the feelings of a lover and sensual desires and passions in us. Devotional songs awaken us to the remembrance of our bond with God. Instead of sensual and worldly desires, they awaken divine qualities in us, and we are able to control our worldly emotions and feelings. It brings peace both to the singer and to the listener.

Amma is not criticizing other kinds of songs. Many find joy in listening to such songs, and people with different personalities and characters inhabit the world. So, people will like different things, and everything has its own significance at their level of being. Amma is not criticizing anything.

When we sing bhajans, we do not aim exclusively for God-realization. There are many other positive aspects to it. Devotional singing and prayers create good vibrations in and around us — there are no thoughts of revenge; there is no enmity; there is only friendliness towards everyone. In prayer, reflection occurs in the minds of the devotees. When a child repeats a word ten times to memorize it, the word becomes firmly embedded in their mind. Likewise, when we sing devotional songs and repeatedly chant God's divine qualities, the divine becomes firmly embedded in our minds, inspiring and energizing our lives.

For whatever reason, it is good to let our tears flow when we pray to God. It will lead us to goodness. Even if the child calls out "fad" instead of "dad," the father will answer. He knows that the child got the word wrong because he doesn't know the right word. God will hear in whatever manner we may pray. God looks only at our hearts. He can't turn away from hearts full of prayer.

Devotional singing brings joy to the mind as well as rest and repose. For us to experience this perfectly, we should feel that "I am nothing; You are everything." This is real prayer. But it may not be so easy to gain this attitude. Darkness will be dispelled only when the sun rises. The perfection of such a state will be attained only when knowledge dawns. But there is no need for us to wait for this to happen. We can continue to cultivate the correct mental attitude within ourselves and move forward. We should never forget that God is our strength. Even our own breath is not in our control. We have heard people say, "I am coming now," as they start to descend the staircase. Before they can even finish their sentence, they collapse and die of a heart attack. Therefore, we should nurture the attitude that, "I am only an instrument in your hands."

Devotional songs and prayers shouldn't be sung or recited only for the gratification of desires. Now, many people see prayer as a means for selfish gain. But we should try to awaken good qualities and positive vibrations through prayer. If man moves forward exclusively satiating only his passions, then rape, looting, and murder will increase. The presence of a police station reduces wrongdoings in society to a large extent, because criminals fear the police. In the case of devotional songs and prayers, on the other hand, it is love and devotion to God that help humanity live with the right values. Such songs and prayers are the practical means to sustain the balance of society, and their tangible positive effects are the real logic or reasoning behind them.

Prayer with good thoughts will cause good vibrations, while prayer with evil thoughts will create bad vibrations. The vibrations generated around a human being will be according to the intention of his prayer. When a person prays for the destruction of his enemy, he will be filled with the vibrations of rage; the world will receive only sensations of rage from him. From each person the world receives vibrations related to the emotional attitudes behind their prayer.

When a man remembers his mother, wife, and daughter, different feelings arise in him. When he thinks of his mother, memories of his mother's love and tenderness are awakened in him. When he thinks of his wife, he is reminded of their relationship as husband and wife and the mutual sharing of their hearts. When he thinks of his child, tenderness overcomes him. All these emotions are in the mind, and they cause and emit different vibrations. Therefore, we should always pray with good thoughts and intentions. Only then will prayer prove to be a positive influence on the individual and on society.

Thoughts are a kind of virus, just like the viruses that cause epidemics. Praying with a heart full of good thoughts, without negative thoughts of revenge and hatred, will not only release us from stress and anxiety, but also create a positive atmosphere both within and without.

If we go near someone suffering from fever, we will also catch it. This is because the flu virus causing the fever will spread to us. When we go to a place where they are bottling perfume, our bodies will also retain some of the fragrance. Likewise, there are subtle vibrations where devotional songs are sung. These vibrations will spread to our aura. If we open our hearts, we will be able to enjoy the devotional songs and become revitalized. If the state of our mind is not favorable, we will not be able to experience the benefits. The interests of people with closed minds will be confined to worldly topics even in such an atmosphere. This is why even when such people go to mahātmās, and the mahātmā makes a resolve for their benefit, they are unable to receive the grace. The frog that lives underneath a lotus flower can neither appreciate its beauty and greatness nor enjoy the fragrance. There is a saying, "Even if the cow's udder is full of milk, the mosquito only longs for blood."

If we run after a bolting cow, it is difficult to catch it. But if we entice the cow with its favorite food, it will come near us. Then we can catch it and tie it up. Likewise, chanting God's name helps us to tame the mind and bring it along with us. At present, our mind is running behind many objects. Nāmajapa, the continuous repetition of divine names, is an easy way to bring the mind under our control and turn it towards God. Even though we say that the creator and creation are one, at present we do not have control over our mind. We should bring the reins of our mind into our hands like the remote control of a TV. We can use the remote to select any channel we want. We are able to discard what we don't need and tune in to what we do need. Likewise, we should be able to control the mind and focus it on what we need. Now, our mind is scattered over many topics and objects. We should be able to bring back the runaway mind. For this, we need japa — we need to repeat the divine names.

45

Question: Are there any particular rules we need to observe to perform spiritual practices?

Amma: Just as there are rules for everything else, there are also certain rules for sādhanā (spiritual practice), meditation, etc. Anybody can sing, but unless you learn classical music, you cannot hold a classical concert. There is theory and structure to classical music that must be learned first. Meditation is where we apply theory in practice, yet if we are not careful, it can harm us. Even though tonic is good for us, it will harm us if we drink up the whole bottle at once instead of the recommended one teaspoon. At the same time, if we drink only two spoonfuls instead of the recommended dosage of five spoonfuls, it will not benefit us. We should take the prescribed dosage. Likewise, we should follow the guru's instructions for meditation.

Some people are allergic to certain drugs. Therefore, an allergy test is usually done before prescribing a drug. Likewise, some forms of sādhanā do not suit everyone. If people follow spiritual practices that do not suit them, they will suffer sleeplessness. Some may become violent and prone to attack others. They may be afflicted by many other physical problems. Some practices can be dangerous if they are not practiced with great care.

However, devotional singing, prayer, and nāmajapa are free from such problems and are suitable for all. But we should be more careful while meditating. For this, a sadhak needs the help of a guru. Even after a rocket has escaped the earth's gravitational attraction, it must burn another thruster to move further into space. Similarly, we need support from the guru to move forward. The ideal sādhanā for a spiritual practitioner is to follow the instructions given by the guru.

We can become either God or a rākṣhasa, Kṛiṣhṇa or Jarāsandha[14]. Both qualities — love and anger — are within us, and our character depends on which quality we nourish. Therefore, we should have good thoughts and not harbor thoughts of revenge and retaliation. We need a clear mind, free from all conflicts. Mental conflicts can be removed through prayer and japa, allowing us to completely forget unnecessary

[14] A mighty but unrighteous king who opposed the righteous Pāṇḍavas in the epic *Mahābhārata* war.

things. Typically, we forget things when our awareness becomes dull. When we regain awareness, we remember them again and feel stressed. But in prayer and japa, we forget with complete awareness. For this, we need to perform disciplined spiritual practices. A guru's help is needed to move forward without any hindrance in our sādhanā.

46

Question: What is the importance of spiritual vows?

Amma: Festivals and spiritual vows are an integral part of our culture. Śhivarātri, Navarātri, Ēkādaśhī, Ṣhaṣhṭhī, Amāvāsyā, etc., are many different days when fasting vows are observed. Such vratas, as vows are called, are very important spiritually, in society, and for our health.

One of the most important uses of vratas is that they help us to bring the mind under our control. When we take a piece of wood to make a boat, it becomes useful only if we can bend it to the required shape. The wood is heated to bend it. Likewise, we can tame or bend the mind to our will by observing vows and other spiritual disciplines. As the shoreline blocks the ocean waves from breaching land, fasting vows serve as a barrier to the waves of the mind. If a river flows in many directions as small streams, we cannot produce electricity from it. When different streams of water are combined and directed into a single flow, the current becomes strong, allowing us to generate electricity. By observing vows, the mind, which tends to wander through many objects, becomes focused and one-pointed.

Vratas also train us to face life's challenges. For example, suppose someone who regularly fasts during Ēkādaśhī has to go without food for an entire day. He will be able to prevail over this situation with ease and comfort.

Once, there was a mahātmā who, even though he was self-realized, would perform pūjās in the morning and sing devotional songs in the evening. A devotee who knew his greatness asked the mahātmā, "Why are you doing all this? Haven't you surmounted all such practices?" The mahātmā replied, "Every day we clean and carefully keep the utensils we use for worship. We should consider our mind and body as utensils for worship."

The journey of our lives can be compared to traveling along a slippery single-log bridge. If we do not take each footstep carefully, we will slip and fall. Similarly, we should live each moment of our lives with awareness. Each word should be spoken with care and every action should be well thought out. Just one careless word or action can lead to great disaster. The cause of the *Mahābhārata* war was one careless word from Pāñchālī. Therefore, we need to have control over our thoughts, words, and actions. Vows and other spiritual observances help us gain such self-control. Maunam – maintaining silence, upavāsa – fasting, and other vows help us to focus our mind and be careful with each of our words and actions. They help to make the mind keen and sharp, and to expand the sphere of our consciousness.

The guru might request a very talkative disciple to take a vow of silence one day a week, or even for an entire week. If the disciple observes the vow of silence regularly, he will not be as talkative as before and will speak only when needed. Regular observance of the vow has made his mind subtle. He has become aware of each thought in his mind. Some people may doubt,

"If silence is so great, then shouldn't people who cannot speak attain salvation? Shouldn't their minds be very alert and aware?" Externally, there is no difference between a mute person and someone observing a vow of silence – neither of them talk – but there is a difference in their silence. The silence of a mute person is natural; they are silent because they cannot speak. It is the silence of helplessness. Whereas a person who takes a vow of silence has the ability to speak, and by remaining silent, he is subduing his own tongue and mind. His mental strength and self-control grow through this observance. We may think that the mind of someone observing silence will still have thoughts even if they do not speak, but they do not lose the energy that is lost from talking. A dam is built across a river to hold back water. Even if there are small waves in the reservoir, no water is lost.

A devotee who used to observe a weekly vow of silence once told Amma, "Amma, one day, I felt very angry with someone. As I started to shout at him, I suddenly realized that I was observing the vow of silence on that day. So, I controlled my mind and kept silent. On another day, when I became angry with someone, I suddenly thought,

"What would I have done if I were observing the vow of silence today?" Then my anger vanished by itself. In this manner, through such vows, we can bring the mind under our control and nurture good qualities within.

For those who cannot control their words, it is better to observe a day of silence. Such vows act like a remote control over the mind and help to conserve our inner energy. When we talk unnecessarily, our strength drains away unnoticed. Excessive chatter or anger dissipates energy through every pore of our body. When we observe a vow of silence, we are conserving our energy. Have you seen small children burning cotton wool with a lens? When light rays pass through the lens, they concentrate on one point, increasing their intensity. Likewise, when the mind is exclusively focused on a single point, it can augment our mental strength. Our mental strength and energy are lost when we allow our mind to travel heedlessly through many thoughts.

We should control not only our words but also our food. It is said that the one who eats once a day is a yōgī, one who eats twice a day is a bhōgī – someone who craves material enjoyment, one who eats thrice a day is a rōgī – he will become a sick person, and one who eats four times a day is a drōhī – a person who is harmful to himself and others. We should eat to remain healthy and to stave off our hunger. But when we indulge in food, we steal from another hungry stomach. Also, when we overeat, our body has to work harder to digest the excess food. Excessive eating does not make us stronger; instead, we lose more energy.

So, we should eat moderately. Half the stomach can be filled with food, a quarter with water, and the rest with air to circulate. The stomach should never be distended. Only then will we be able to breathe rhythmically. Excessive eating will upset the rhythm of breathing.

Every machine requires rest. If we continuously run a mixer or grinder for twenty-four hours, its motor will burn out. Likewise, the body, mind, and internal organs also need rest. Fasting makes this possible as it helps eliminate waste and cleanses the small and large intestines. The mind and body will both benefit from one day of food fasting and one day of silence.

Success in life depends on a person's alert awareness. All spiritual practices are intended to awaken and uplift our level of awareness. If we can remain aware of each thought and action, our mind and body will come under our control. Life will be filled with success, joy, and peace.

When we observe vratas (vows) with discipline and regularity, we gradually become cleansed of our mental impurities; our mind becomes pure, and our mental strength increases. Each time we give in to bad habits and temptations, our mental strength weakens, and the mind becomes turbulent. Conversely, each time we overcome temptations, our mind becomes stronger, more settled, and at peace.

47

Question: What is the benefit of pilgrimages?

Amma: Pilgrimages help release the mind from worldly matters and focus it on God, even if only for a short while. They provide an opportunity to gain self-control through the disciplined observance of vows and the practice of renunciation during travel. Pilgrimages also allow us to utilize the positive vibrations present in holy places to reflect upon God. Most importantly, we undertake pilgrimages to purify the mind. Everything else is in vain if we do not achieve purity of mind.

Pilgrimages are a part of our culture. After reaching a certain age, our ancestors used to pass on their wealth to their children or other relatives and leave for pilgrimages. They would walk to Kashi or the Himalayas. If their legs became tired, they would rest for a while somewhere. They would meditate, eat whatever they received as alms, and continue their journey, sleeping underneath trees or in wayside inns. They would continue on their journey with the belief that they will attain liberation if they die in Kashi. Their goal was to attain liberation, so they had no interest in anything else. Just as food becomes tasteless and even sweetness feels bitter when one has a fever, for them, the pilgrimage was a form of constant meditation.

But today, even before starting a pilgrimage, most people book an AC room in a hotel. From the moment they set out, they talk about family and society, and these discussions continue even when they return. In the midst of all this, they forget to think about God. They may bathe in many holy waters, visit many great temples, and make many offerings, but they will receive the fruit of their actions only if they attune their hearts to God. If liberation could be achieved simply by visiting a holy place, wouldn't all the merchants there also have attained liberation?

When it rains, a lot of water falls on the earth, making it wet and muddy, which people find inconvenient. But an oyster shell in the ocean waits with longing to receive even a single drop of rain, so that it can transform the raindrop into a priceless pearl. Similarly, God constantly showers grace upon us, but the results will depend on how we assimilate it.

We are willing to wait at a bus stop for as long as it takes for the bus to arrive, and we do not hesitate to spend an entire day waiting in the corridors of a court of law. But we do not display any patience when we go to an ashram or a temple. When we go to holy places, we should spend some time remembering God. We should chant God's name, meditate, or perform some selfless action. We must decrease our luxuries and trim down our opulent lifestyle. Only then will our actions bear fruit.

Faith is the foundation for everything. If there is faith and love, any water will become holy. Do you know the story of Pākkanār? Once, a brahmin decided to go to Kashi, bathe in the river Ganga, and pray at the temple of Kashi Vishwanath. He asked Pākkanār to come along with him. Pākkanār was unable to go but said, "As you are going anyway, it will be very helpful if you can take my staff, dip it in the Ganga and bring it back to me." The brahmin agreed and took the staff along with him. He reached Kashi, but the river's current swept away Pākkanār's staff as he bathed in the Ganga. When he returned, the brahmin told Pākkanār that he had lost the staff. Pākkanār said, "Don't worry, I will retrieve the lost staff." Pākkanār dove into the water of his pond and came up with the very same staff. Then he told the brahmin, "If you have faith, any water becomes the water of the holy Ganga. If not, even the waters of the Ganga and the Yamuna remain just water."

This does not mean that holy places and sacred waters are not special. They may be places where mahātmās once lived, or where gurus and gurukulas once existed. The devotion-soaked thoughts of devotees, the chanting of mantras, and the singing of God's names will also have purified the place. The vibrations of such places are conducive to performing spiritual practices and immersing oneself in thoughts of God. But if pilgrimages turn into picnics or mere routine, we will not get the real benefit. We must not forget that remembering God, having faith, and maintaining a pure heart are paramount.

We have seen the flow of pilgrims to Sabarimala during the pilgrimage season in November and December. Some may ask, why is it necessary to wear black clothes, balance the bundled offering on the head, and set out in the direction of the temple? Isn't devotion an inner experience, a bliss within? It is true that devotion is supreme love for God. The indications of devotion are an attitude of surrender or total commitment, and an unbroken remembrance of God. But this is our goal, and we have not yet attained the goal. Therefore, we need to observe rituals and vows and maintain disciplined spiritual practice. Just as a plane must taxi on the runway before taking off into the sky, these observances serve a similar purpose.

Temple rituals, observances, vows, and pilgrimages are paths to the goal of prēma-bhakti, which is perfect devotion based on pure love for God. Just as the stars lose their prominence once the sun rises high in the sky, traditions lose their importance once we achieve pure love. A road is needed for vehicles and human beings to travel, but birds flying up in the sky do not need a road. Likewise, once we attain the goal of pure love, traditions are no longer that important.

More than a traditional temple visit, the pilgrimage to Sabarimala is one of penance, austerity, and vows. Through discernment and control of the desires arising in our mind, vows help us gain mastery over the mind and strengthen it.

Whatever spiritual path we follow, constant and disciplined spiritual practice is necessary to progress. The forty-one days of austerity and vows that are part of the Sabarimala pilgrimage help to turn the mind inward, keeping it concentrated on God. Our body and mind are also purified. We should not return to our old habits as soon as the forty-one-day period is over because that would not benefit us. We should be able to maintain the good habits we followed during those forty-one days of vows. But many people do not pay much attention to this and slide back into their old ways. When they do that, the purpose of these vows and worship is not fulfilled. As we take our lives forward, we should turn the saṁskāras (positive impressions in our mind) and the mental strength and control gained through such vows into stepping stones. Only then will temple worship, vows, and pilgrimages lead to the fulfillment of our lives.

48

Question: Kṛiṣhṇa says in the Bhagavad Gītā that we only have the right to do actions but not to their fruit. Doesn't this mean that we should work but not ask for our wages?

Amma: This is not the right understanding. When the Lord says that we have no right to the fruits of our actions, he means that we have no control over them. He does not say that we do not deserve them. However, when we work for spiritual progress, our aim is inner cleansing, not external gain.

When we do any action, the result may not be according to our expectations. Then the one who has acted with his hopes pinned on the fruits of his actions will experience sorrow and disappointment. Our chances of success are higher when we perform any action with our full attention and focus directed on the action itself.

This is the meaning behind Bhagavān's words. He does not mean that we should work without taking any wages. He asks us to act without desire so that we achieve the best results.

Some people ask, 'How is it possible to act without desiring the fruits of our actions?' Do not become anxious thinking about the fruits of your actions; act with care and focus. You will definitely receive the fruits. A child studying for exams need not worry about whether they will pass or fail. It is enough that they study thoroughly. An architect building a house should not distress themselves wondering whether it will collapse; instead, they should concentrate on building it according to plan.

If we perform our actions with full awareness, we will definitely receive their fruits. Instead, if we keep thinking of the fruits, we will feel anxious even while performing our actions and also while receiving their fruits. When we sow a seed, it may sprout or it may not. If the rain fails us, we can dig a well and water the plant. In this way, we can ensure its growth. But despite all our efforts, there is no guarantee that we will be able to reap a good harvest. When it is time for harvesting, floods or strong winds may destroy the crop.

This is the nature of the world. If we live with this knowledge, we will not have sorrow. This is why Bhagavān says, "Perform your actions; the result is in His hands. Do not become distraught and anxious." We may strive hard, but God's grace is also needed for a good harvest. The Lord does not advise us to work without asking for or receiving remuneration. No one can prophesy with certainty what the fruits of any action will be. This is why the Lord says that you have no authority over the fruits of your actions. The Lord advises us in this manner so that we may live a life free of sorrow. It does not mean we should only work and not ask for wages.

If a farmer sells good rice that is sorted and free of stones, everyone will buy it. But if he desires inordinate profit and adulterates it, he will face punishment – if not today, then tomorrow. His mind will also be unsettled. Therefore, we should act with care and sincerity, with the awareness that, "I am only an instrument in God's hands."

When we say, "become an instrument in God's hands," it does not mean that we should work like a robot or a slave. The attitude of being an instrument in God's hand is the natural and spontaneous expression of a devotee's love for the Lord. When we become an instrument in the Lord's hands, we experience God's love. It inspires us to work with insight and total commitment. When we offer our actions to God, we will try to do them to the best of our abilities and strive for perfection. Through this, we achieve skill in action.

If we perform actions while desiring their fruits, the merits and demerits of our actions will bind us. On the other hand, if we act with skill and surrender, and without yearning for the fruits of our actions, then our actions will not bind us. One must be free from attachments to succeed in any field of action. Often it is our attachment to people and objects that stand as barriers to doing the right action. We can see many such examples around us. Even a very experienced surgeon will not have the courage to operate on his own wife or daughter. Even a just judge would not be ready to write the judgment for their own child, the prime suspect accused in a murder. From this, we can understand that our attachments and aversions towards individuals and objects influence our capability to act.

Through karma yōga (the path of selfless action), Bhagavān shows us the most practical and efficient way to perform actions, which also leads us forward on the path to liberation, which is our supreme goal.

49

Question: What is the role of action and the fruit of action in our life?

Amma: Two things happen in our life: one, we act, and two, we experience the fruits of our actions. Life will be filled with peace if we learn the right attitude for performing our actions and for accepting the fruits of our actions. We will be able to circumvent many of the problems and difficulties of life.

It is common in life that sometimes our efforts do not bear fruit despite trying with all our strength and might, while at other times, our efforts succeed without much difficulty. What is the reason for this? This happens because the fruits of our previous actions influence the effectiveness of our present efforts. Therefore, we should be very careful about how we act today. Only then will we have a bright tomorrow.

This is why each action, each word, and each look should be done with awareness. Each has its own effect. The good actions we perform now will give us good experiences in the future. Our wrong actions come back to us later as experiences of sorrow. Fate is the result of our own actions. Yesterday's actions become tomorrow's fate. If today's actions are pure, tomorrow's fate will favor us.

Time and place are not barriers to the fruits of our actions. It is like the law of the land. If one commits a crime, even if he goes and hides in some remote corner of the country, the police will go after him, find him, and give him fair punishment. Similarly, whether we live in this world or any other world, the fruits of our actions will follow us. But no one can say for sure when and how each person will experience them. The ways of karma are very mysterious and hidden.

None can run away from his karma-phala (fruits of actions). We will have to experience the merits of our good actions and the demerits of our wrong actions in the future. However, we should not sit idle saying that all that happens is fated to happen. Effort has its own significance. If we fall sick, we take medicine and thereby reduce the intensity of suffering. Likewise, with the right effort and good deeds, we can reduce the intensity of the suffering we are meant to experience.

We can overcome the fruits of our negative actions through good deeds. Even if we throw a stone up into the sky, we can catch it before it falls back and hits us. Or we can move away from the spot. Through his penance, Mārkaṇḍēya received a longer life span. Through penance, Sāvitrī was able to bring Satyavān back to life.[15] The robber Ratnākara was transformed into sage Vālmīki by chanting the Lord's name. Likewise, through effort and good deeds, we can reduce the burden of our suffering and overcome it.

The joy and sorrow we experience now result from our actions done in this life and in our previous lives. Even this human body is the result of our past deeds. Therefore, if our actions are performed in the right manner with faith,

---

[15] The pure and devoted Sāvitrī married Satyavān despite his foretold early death. Through her steadfast devotion, she persuaded Yama, the god of death, to restore Satyavān's life.

awareness, and intelligence, we can lead a contented life. This does not mean that we will not experience sorrow in our life. Joy and sorrow are the nature of life. Yet, if we perform our actions with discernment, we can find happiness in life.

50

Question: Are the traditions of Hinduism logical?

Amma: A breastfeeding infant will not be able to digest meat; it will make them sick. They should be fed simple food, easy to digest. Likewise, we should reach out to each person at their level and lead them from where they currently stand. Because of this, we find in Sanātana Dharma what is suitable for every level. We should explain things to people based on their physical, mental, and intellectual constitution. Some traditional practices may seem primitive or crude, however, if we look at them with logic and reason, we will understand their practicality. It is not wrong to say that practicability is the foundation of Sanātana Dharma. If we reflect on a deep and subtle level, we will gain insight into the practical benefits of what might seem illogical on a superficial level.

We do not require intellectual gymnastics. We need practical logic that benefits humanity. There is a saying that if you lie, your eyes will shatter. Our intellect will say that if this were true, you would see only blind people in this world. Yet, when a small child hears this, they will refrain from lying. If we tell a child watching TV, "Child, come, I will give you immortality," they will not come but insist that watching TV gives them joy. But if you say, "Run, there is a snake in the room," they will not hesitate but immediately run out. The words were the catalyst that helped to bring the child to the goal. Here, we focus not on logic but on the practical benefits. Some Hindu traditions may seem to be wrong practices at first sight. But if we look closely, we will see the many practical benefits they have for people. If any practices harm society, the Hindu religion has the breadth of vision to rectify or remove them.

51

Question: How did wrong practices come into being?

Amma: Sanātana Dharma is very logical. It does not prohibit questioning. It encourages questions.

Most of its scriptural texts came into existence as the answers to questions from serious seekers. Sanātana Dharma does not ask us to believe anything unquestioningly. We feel many traditional practices are wrong or misguided (anāchāram) because we do not understand the spiritual principles or the foundational knowledge behind those practices. The remedy to this is to understand the religious principles in their essence.

In the Christian and Muslim faiths, children are taught about their religion from a very early age; they are required to go to their churches and mosques. As a result, they know their religious principles and practices. However, in Hinduism, there are no such compulsions at present. Because of this, the majority of Hindus have no spiritual knowledge or awareness. Some believe that the superstitions and wrong practices that developed through the ages are a part of the Hindu religion and accept them as such. Some others consider them illogical and reject them. No one tries to understand the real meaning of the words of the ancient sages. Even if a few people try to understand, the opportunities to gain such knowledge are sparse. In earlier days, the fundamental understanding of religion was disseminated through temples. Nowadays, no one in the temples is able to impart such knowledge.

Temple authorities should make arrangements to impart spiritual knowledge to those who visit the temples. They should hold awareness classes to nourish our culture. Opportunities for such classes should be created within the temple precincts. Books that explain spiritual principles should be sold at concessional rates. The income received by the temples should be used for these purposes. If this is done, people will be able to understand and imbibe the essential principles of Sanātana Dharma correctly. Once knowledge is gained, superstitions and wrong practices will become fewer and fewer in society.

52

Question: Some people say that astrology is a superstitious belief. Is astrology helpful in facing life's problems?

Amma: Many people seek solace in jyōtiṣha (Vedic astrology) to alleviate their fears and anxiety about the future. Many people obsess over matters such as their children's marriage, their business, job promotions, etc. The fruits of our past actions come back to us as pain and pleasure. To an extent, astrology may be able to give some pointers in this regard. But it will not be able to eradicate our demerits completely. Therefore, we should develop a mind that can overcome the problems that arise in life.

Once, a mahātmā gave two statues to a king and said, "Take good care of these statues. When they break, disasters in the form of war, drought or floods may occur in the kingdom." The king entrusted one of his attendants with the two statues and made him responsible for storing them safely. However, one day, one of them broke. The attendant informed the king, and the furious king had him shut up in prison. A few days later, a large army led by the neighboring king attacked the kingdom. The king's anger blazed high, and he ordered the attendant to be hung. He asked the man whether he had any dying wish, and the man replied, "Before I die, allow me to also break the other statue." "Why do you wish this?" asked the king. The attendant replied, "You pronounced the death sentence on me because one of the statues broke. The other statue should not be the reason for the death of another innocent. The mahātmā who gifted you the two statues only said bad times would occur when a statue breaks. He did not say that hard times would come because a statue broke. The statue broke as a sign for the impending invasion. The signal you received should have prompted you to prepare to face the enemy army." Hearing these words, the king realized his mistake and released the attendant from all punishment.

Horoscopes and omens only give signals of the impending joys and sorrows one will experience in life. There is no use in finding fault with the planets or God for the hardships we go through in life. Let us try to make today's actions good. In proportion to the good actions we perform in the present, the future will be benevolent towards us.

We should try to prevent adverse circumstances. But if we are unable to do so, we should develop a mind that accepts whatever happens in our life as the will of God. Then we can experience peace and calm in our lives.

53

Question: What is the role of ātmā-kṛipā, the grace of one's own self, in our life?

Amma: God is constantly showering his grace upon us. But to utilize it, we need ātmā-kṛipā, the grace of our own self. What is the use of lamenting that the sun does not give me light if I tightly shut all the doors and windows in the morning? The sun shines its light everywhere. We only need to open the doors to receive it. Likewise, God is constantly showering his grace upon us. To receive his grace, we should open the closed doors of our heart. Therefore, over and above God's grace, we should first receive the grace of our own mind.

In India, children are given moderation marks to pass exams. Even though anyone can get those grace marks, there is a certain minimum number of marks that a child must earn through their own effort in order to become eligible. Those who do not study will not get the benefit of moderation. Likewise, effort is also needed on our part.

God is not a mere judge sitting there to give the verdict of good fruits for good actions and bad fruits for wrong actions. God is above everything, the epitome of grace. He is a treasure trove of grace who forgives our faults and grants us his grace. But he can shower his grace upon us and save us only if there is at least a little bit of effort on our part. If we don't make an effort, we won't be able to accept the grace that God, the embodiment of compassion, showers on us. If we are unable to receive God's grace, it is not his fault — it is our fault.

Lord Kṛiṣhṇa wanted to prevent the *Mahābhārata* war and the destruction of the Kauravas. He pleaded with Duryōdhana to give at least one house to the Pāṇḍavas. But with arrogance and enmity, Duryōdhana rejected his plea. The result was total destruction. Duryōdhana lacked ātmākṛipā to accept the Lord's grace.

We find advertisements in newspapers for hiring people. They enumerate the needed qualifications, such as degree and character certificates, height, weight, etc. However, during the interviews it was found that even if a candidate had all the right qualifications and answered all the questions, some were not chosen for the job. On the other hand, other candidates who were unable to answer all the questions were given the job. The reason for this is that the interviewer felt empathy towards them. This is God's grace.

Our good actions shape us into vessels fit to receive God's grace. Therefore, to receive God's grace, we first need to cultivate our own grace.

54

Question: Does the Hindu religion have the concept of everlasting hell?

Amma: Sanātana Dharma views everyone as divine; hence, there is no such concept as an everlasting hell. There is another reason why the Hindu religion does not have an everlasting hell. Actions, whether good or bad, cannot give everlasting results. This is because both the action and the fruits of action are limited. A jīva (individual soul) lives in heaven or hell only for the time needed to experience their accumulated merits or demerits, which are the results of their past actions. Once it has finished experiencing the fruits of its actions, the jīva will receive its next birth. It may be on this earth or in some other world.

Sanātana Dharma teaches us that even if we have committed the most heinous sin, through good thoughts and good actions, we can purify ourselves and finally realize God. When the robber Ratnākara obeyed the advice of the sages, he became sage Vālmīki (author of the Rāmāyaṇa epic). Even someone who has committed many crimes can save themselves through sincere penitence. There is no sin that cannot be washed away by the tears of repentance, but it should not be like an elephant's bath. An elephant will bathe in a river, climb back onto the river bank and, in a short while, start throwing dust all over its body. Many people are like this.

As we move forward in life, we may have done many wrongs, but my children should not dwell on them and lose their strength. We should remember that we fall to the ground only to pick ourselves up again. We shouldn't lie there, thinking the ground is comfortable, nor should we break down by obsessing over the fact that we have fallen. Instead, we should strive to get up and move forward.

When we write with a pencil on paper, we can erase mistakes and write correctly. But if we repeatedly make mistakes and try to rub them away, the paper may tear. Likewise, if we persist in committing wrongs, we move toward our own destruction. Therefore, my children should strive not to repeat their mistakes and should remain constantly aware.

55

Question: Some people say that women should not chant the Lalitā Sahasranāma. It is also said that we incur sin if we make any mistakes in pronunciation while chanting. Is there any basis for these claims?

Amma: Isn't Śhrī Lalitā Dēvī in the form of a woman? If women cannot chant her names, then who else should chant them? In the phala-śhruti – the description of the results obtained from recitation of a chant – it has not been stated that women should not chant Lalitā Dēvī's names. Then on what basis are these people making such claims?

Superstitions spread by selfish minds have taken hold and still remain strong in many places. There have been some small changes for the better, but there is so much more that needs changing. It is indeed surprising that in this day and age, there are still people who believe that women should not chant Dēvī's mantra or Dēvī's Sahasranāma (thousand names). 'Ōm śhrī mātrē namaḥ — I offer adorations to my mother."[16] Do we need to learn classical music to call out to our own mother? Isn't the mother all forgiving and forbearing? The mother who gives birth will forgive all the mistakes of her child. When this is so, why do we think that Dēvī, the very personification of love, will not forgive the mistakes of her devotees? Dēvī doesn't look at what we say but at the bhāva, the feeling of our heart. She is pleased when she sees our heart's innocence.

How can we learn anything without making mistakes? Are all people born as jñānis, with perfect knowledge? People fall many times before they finally get onto the right path. How can they reach perfection if we abandon them with the first mistake they make? Does Dēvī not have a heart expansive enough to understand this? Those pundits who have ruled, "It is a sin to chant the mantras wrong, and you will have to go to hell, if you do so," have themselves made many mistakes while learning those mantras. If that were true, think of how many times they themselves would have to go to hell. Nevertheless, each one of us should try not to make mistakes in our

---

[16] First name of the *Lalitā Sahasranāma*, the thousand names of the Divine Mother.

pronunciation while chanting the Sahasranāma; therefore, it is ideal to read the mantras from a book while chanting.

56

Question: In this world, some are healthy, and some are sick. Some are rich, while others are poor. Some are beautiful, while others are ugly. Is God partial?

Amma: We cannot blame God for such inequality; the fault lies with us. If our actions are pure, the results or fruits of our actions will also be ideal. The sorrows we have to experience in this present life are the result of our actions done in previous lifetimes. There is no use in blaming God. Moreover, although we have increased our harvest tenfold using genetically modified seeds, artificial fertilizers, and chemical pesticides, the goodness in grains and vegetables has become considerably less. Traces of poison enter the bodies of those who eat them. They and the children born to those who eat the food produced in this manner become sick. Our selfishness is the reason for such a state of affairs. We cannot blame God for this.

Once, a supervisor gave his two workers the task of breaking stones. One worker was strong, and the other weak. After a few days, the supervisor came to inspect their work. He pointed to two rocks and asked them to break the rocks with a sledgehammer. The strong man hit his rock ten times but the rock refused to yield. The weak man had to hit his rock only twice before it split into two. The strong man asked, "How could you break this rock with only two blows?" The other replied, "I had already hit it many times before." Likewise, if life seems easy for some and difficult for others today, it is the result of their previous actions. Our progress today is the fruit of the good actions we performed yesterday. For it to be sustained tomorrow, we should do good actions today. Otherwise, tomorrow, we will have to experience sorrow.

When we see someone in trouble, we should not abandon him or remain indifferent, considering it his karma-phala — the fruits of his own actions. Instead, we should think that helping him is our dharma — our duty and responsibility. If we show compassion to the suffering today, we will not have to suffer tomorrow. By helping someone out of a ditch today, we can save ourselves from a fall tomorrow.

In a way, the sorrow we have to experience in this present life is a blessing from God as it helps us to remember him. We have seen people who have never even once called out to God, turning to him and following the path of dharma when sorrow overtakes them. Through this, they are able to gain release from the sorrows which are the fruits of previous actions.

57

Question: The story of Kṛiṣhṇa stealing the clothes of the gōpīs and performing the rāsa-līlā with them is portrayed as 'indecent' by some people.

Amma: If someone portrays the divine sport of the Lord with the gōpīs (the milkmaids of Vṛindāvan) as obscene, it reveals the depravity of their mind. How can a normal mind view a seven- or eight-year-old child this way? This was the Lord's age at the time of the rāsa-līlā[17]. Now, we are attached to our body, mind, and intellect. Only when we

[17] Mystic dance of divine love in which Lord Kṛiṣhṇa manifested as many identical forms of himself as there

free ourselves from the constraints of shame and prudery caused by such attachment can we connect with the paramātman – the supreme self. We will experience true bliss only when our mind becomes attached to the paramātman. The only aim of the Lord was to make everyone blissful. This joy is not what you gain from external objects but the blissful experience of our true self. The Lord lifted the gōpīs to this level. This is possible only when one is no longer aware of the physical body. This was the Lord's intention. The spiritual principle behind stealing their clothes is to uplift them from their identification of themselves with their bodies. They are able to experience the bliss of the self only if they abandon their identification with the body. This is the rāsa-līlā.

It was the gōpīs' hearts that Kṛiṣhṇa stole. This is why he is called 'chitta-chōra' – the stealer of hearts. Even today, he steals the hearts of many.

He did not sit quietly saying that I am God and will do only certain things. He demonstrated how to live according to each situation. He played all his roles well, without any blemish. To know

---

were gōpīs, thus leading each gōpī to believe he was dancing with her alone.

him, we should reflect on his stories with an open mind. Those who criticize the Lord do not know that they are revealing their minds' capricious and unstable nature.

58

Question: It is said that Śhrī Kṛiṣhṇa had sixteen thousand and eight wives. How can this be explained?

Amma: The Lord was the King of Dvārakā. In those days, kings had more than one wife. Lord Kṛiṣhṇa had eight. The Lord did not marry the other sixteen thousand women just to make them his wives; they had been enslaved and imprisoned by Narakāsura. The Lord slew Narakāsura and freed them. But having been forced to live in Narakāsura's prison, the women knew that no one would accept them and that they would never have lives of their own. So, they decided to kill themselves. Knowing their thoughts and recognizing their plight, the Lord consoled and accepted them in marriage, giving them respectability in society. Thus, he protected the women and gave them a new life. We can only bow down before such a great heart.

59

Question: Why are birds and animals worshiped in the Hindu religion?

Amma: Sanātana Dharma sees divine consciousness in everything, both animate and inanimate. Consequently, a culture developed in which everything is viewed with honor and respect. The ancient ṛiṣhis did not see birds and animals as unworthy or inferior; they saw them as manifest forms of God. Temples were built for animals, birds, trees, rivers, mountains, and other beings, whether animate or inanimate. Snakes, spiders, and even lizards were given a place in temple worship. Sanātana Dharma teaches us that for a human life to reach perfection, it needs the blessings of even an ant. In the Bhāgavatam, we can read the story of the avadhūta who accepted twenty-four teachers from nature, including birds and animals. Therefore, we should always maintain the humility, curiosity, and eagerness of a beginner, as we have lessons to learn from everything.

The ṛiṣhis saw divine consciousness even in inert objects. They sang, "sarvaṁ brahmamayaṁ rē rē sarvaṁ brahmamayaṁ — everything is imbued with divine consciousness." Science tells us that everything is energy; the scientific theories are also moving towards the principle of oneness. The people of Bhārat who had faith in the words of the sages saw God in everything and bowed their heads in devotion.

Amma remembers certain incidents from her childhood. Even if she accidentally stepped on a piece of paper while she was sweeping, Amma would bend down, touch it with reverence, and fold her palms in prayer. Otherwise, my mother would beat me. She would tell me, "It's not just a piece of paper; it's Dēvī Sarasvatī – the goddess of learning." Also, if we stepped on cow manure, we had to touch it with reverence and pray with folded palms. Cow manure is fertilizer. Grass grows from it and is given as fodder to the cows. We then use the milk that the cow gives. We were also not supposed to step on the threshold of the house (considered inauspicious). If we did, we had to touch it and pray.

Such habits are needed to take us forward from where we stand. When we take this view, everything has value. There is nothing to reject. 'Mithya' is not that which doesn't exist; it is that which undergoes change. This is why we should view everything with respect and reverence. This is what Sanātana Dharma teaches us.

60

Question: Aren't many of the Hindu religion's traditions primitive, including the worship of birds and animals?

Amma: At first glance, many of the Hindu religion's traditions may seem primitive, but if we study their subtle essence, we will realize that noble ideals and intentions underlie these rituals. If the Hindu religion seems primitive it is not correctly understood. The Hindu religion is suitable for every age and can include and accept all reforms and progressive approaches. Its heart is ever-expansive.

The words of the ancient sages and mahātmās who saw divine consciousness pervading everything are the inspiration behind the great traditions of Sanātana Dharma. They told us to respect and revere everything in creation.

Man's very existence depends on nature and its flora and fauna. This in itself is reason enough for us to love and show our respect for them. A child grows up drinking its mother's breast milk.

The child is indebted to its mother for its life. Humanity should have the same mother-and-child relationship with each living creature in nature. This realization motivated us to worship the living beings around us.

All the civilizations that developed in Bhārat were connected to rivers and forests. We also know how integral they are to human existence. Our ancestors never felt the need to dominate nature; instead, they had an attitude of worship born out of love. This is why we can see numerous mantras praising nature in the *Vēdas*. This worship helped humanity understand that they were a part of nature, thus refraining from exploiting and destroying it.

This universe is God's creation. If God is perfect, then his creation is also perfect. If we light a thousand lamps from a single lamp, all the thousand flames will be as perfect as the first one. How can we set one aside, saying that it is imperfect? Looking at the world in this manner, we cannot say that anything in this universe which God permeates is lowly or debased and discriminate against it. Therefore, the culture of this land became one of respect and worship – worship of birds, animals, trees, mountains, forests, and all things sentient and insentient. The Hindu religion teaches that nothing in this universe is unworthy of worship. It teaches us to understand that we are a part of nature and not to exploit nature.

'Why do we worship cows? Why do we worship snakes? Does God reside in these creatures?' Many people ask such questions. When you go to foreign countries, you can see the tenderness they lavish on their pet cats and dogs. They do not show such love even towards their own children. The pain they undergo when their pet dies may be greater than if their husband died. So many people come to Amma and burst out crying because their pet animals died. They do not wonder where their father, mother, husband, wife, or children went after death. But if their cat died, they want to know where its soul went. So strong is their love for that animal.

But this love stems from attachment. If ordinary people can love so intensely, think of the boundless love that the sages and mahātmās had for all of creation and for all creatures in which they perceived God. Because they see God in everything, their lives are entirely blissful; they do not have any sorrow. They recommended many paths to uplift others and bring them into this all-encompassing vision of oneness. One of these paths is to develop a heart that sees all creatures as God and loves them. Traditions that help us to reach this goal cannot be rejected. As God exists in all beings, we should see each and every being in nature — both sentient and insentient —as God and worship them.

61

Question: Many people criticize the Hindu religion for its practice of animal sacrifice. Isn't what they say true?

Amma: Some people are unable to see the transformation that occurs in those who perform religious practices in accordance with the underlying religious principles; they can only see shortcomings. They criticize Hinduism by pointing to the practice of animal sacrifices that were once performed in the name of religion. Listening to them, we will think that the Hindu religion consists only of animal sacrifice. They have nothing to say about the killing of animals in other religions. When asked to sacrifice the animal of the ego, in their ignorance, some people sacrificed animals. Millions of animals are killed and eaten every year. How many people criticize this? Doesn't modern man, said to be knowledgeable, perform human sacrifices? How many people are being murdered in the name of religion and politics? Even though we claim to have advanced from our ancestors' way of life, we have not. The progress we are now pointing at is leading us to another downfall. We must view matters comprehensively to know this. We must have an aerial view. When we look from the ground, we will see only one side of the matter.

Amma does not agree at all with the practice of animal sacrifice in the name of pleasing God. It is not possible for anyone with a heart to witness the agony of the animal as it dies writhing in pain. It is not right to blame God, who is the embodiment of love and compassion, for the practice of animal sacrifice. Sanātana Dharma teaches that non-violence is the supreme dharma. It is sad and disturbing to see innocent animals being mercilessly slaughtered. God will never approve of animal slaughter. We must not take even one life in the name of God. This is Amma's only request to everyone.

It is true that bali — sacrifice — is mentioned in the karma kāṇḍa (ritualistic portion) of the *Vēdas*, but we should observe the sacrifice, knowing the real principle behind it. The real meaning behind animal sacrifice is this: we sacrifice our animal mind and the ego that causes it. Real sacrifice is when we slice off our own ego using the sword of knowledge. Through this, the Lord and his devotee become one.

Long ago, forest dwellers had no other means of livelihood but hunting. They assuaged their hunger by eating the meat of the animals they hunted. They also offered their favorite food to God. We cannot say that killing and eating animals when they found no other way to stay alive was wrong. But when animals are sacrificed to gain personal desires, it cannot be justified in any manner.

These cruel malpractices result from ignorance of the foundational knowledge of religion and God. Therefore, we need to make people aware of their meaninglessness.

Those who desired to eat meat conducted animal sacrifices and used God as a screen behind which they gratified their desire. People also performed animal sacrifices to fulfill specific purposes. They see God, the creator and controller of this universe, merely as an agent who accepts small gifts and grants them their specific desires. This is tamasic worship — worship born out of ignorance. The custom of sacrificing animals is prevalent in many religions in many parts of the world. When such sacrifice is offered, one may temporarily gain the intended result, but one thing is sure: they will have to experience the fruits of their violent actions later in time.

When we talk about animal sacrifice, we should also reflect upon the terrible cruelties shown to animals in order to eat meat. Humans show extreme cruelty to animals as they are taken to slaughterhouses and also in the ways in which they are killed. They are injected with chemicals to make their flesh tender and heavier. This is an example of man falling even lower than animals in pursuit of selfish gratification. Animals experience the same emotions as humans — fear, pain, sorrow, happiness, love, and loyalty. When another living being endures pain due to our actions, their vibrations of sorrow will return to the ones responsible for causing the pain, and become the cause of our own sorrow over time.

Good and evil exist within everyone's heart. Of the two, the quality that we nourish will gain strength. We can either embody goodness or personify evil — both possibilities are within us. One can be either Kṛiṣhṇa or Kaṁsa, Rāma or Rāvaṇa.

The selfishness and ego inhabiting our hearts should leave us, and love and compassion should take their place. We should take as noble role models King Śhibi, who was willing to give up his own life to save that of a dove, Śhrī Buddha, who was ready to sacrifice himself for the sake of a lamb, and Yudhishthira, who was willing to give up heaven for the sake of a dog. We should grow and evolve to a state in which we can see even an ant as our own self and thus revere and worship it. This should be our goal when we worship God.

62

Question: Why is a monkey worshiped as God in the Hindu religion?

Amma: Sanātana Dharma teaches us to see not just a monkey but everything in nature as God and to love and serve all. God is not an individual who sits on a golden throne up in the sky; he is the divine consciousness that permeates every being. This nature we see in front of our eyes is a manifest form of God. His light shines equally through the big and small; it shines through the pillars and a speck of rusted iron, through a blade of grass and a worm, through all the birds and animals, humanity, and even through inert objects. When that is so, what is wrong with seeing God in a monkey and worshiping it?

The monkey is a symbol of the human mind. Isn't it said that monkeys were the forefathers of humans? When we lie inside the womb, we have the shape of a monkey. Even after taking birth, the monkey mind does not leave us.

Ordinary monkeys leap from one tree branch to another. Similarly, a man's mind is in Bhārat this second, then the next second, it is in the United States. The very next second, it will reach the Moon. From there, it will jump to the Sun and Mars. The methods of worship in the Hindu religion are meant to focus this monkey mind on one point. Many types of worship have been advised as suitable for different mental predispositions. The mind is like an uncontrolled monkey when it jumps according to the tune of the vāsanās (latent tendencies) and desires that fill the mind.

When the mind grasps the spiritual principles, it becomes imbued with devotion and discernment, achieves self-control, becomes an instrument in God's hands, and is illumined with the divine consciousness. This is the principle behind the monkey Hanumān becoming the devoted servant of Śhrī Rāma, and later being elevated to the status of God, worthy of worship.

Hanumān shows us that we can become God by chanting the divine names and practicing dāsya-bhakti, which means surrendering oneself to God's service. Awake and asleep, Hanumān had only one thought: "Śhrī Rāma." Hanumān constantly chanted Rāma's name. It is said that Rāma's name resounded through each hair follicle on Hanumān's body and that Śhrī Rāma's form filled Hanumān's heart. He could only see Śhrī Rāma in everyone. He even wanted to see Śhrī Kṛiṣhṇa in the form of Śhrī Rāma. Hanumān's devotion to Rāma was strong and unshakeable. He excelled in all ideal qualities: an acute sense of responsibility, unwavering enthusiasm, courage, fearlessness, celibacy, unshakeable faith, dedication, surrender, and more. Through such ideal devotion and spiritual discipline, Hanumān grew from the status of a mere monkey to the status of a god, worshiped by others.

"When I think of myself as the body, I am your servant; when I think of myself as an individual soul, I am a part of you; when I think of myself as the ātman, you and I are one," says Hanumān to Rāma. Hanumān's story teaches us that if we have the same disciplined devotion as he had towards his Lord and are ready to chant the divine name constantly, we will gain God's vision and rise to the level of God. When we worship Hanumān, his ideal qualities will gradually be reflected in us.

Hanumān shows us that we can even overcome death by chanting Rāma's name. Once, a sage stood in the waters of a river and filled his cupped hands with water to perform his evening worship. A Gandharva (celestial being) traveling through the sky spat down, and the spit fell into the water held in the sage's hands. The sage felt sad and angry. He went to Śhrī Rāma and asked him to deliver justice by slaying the Gandharva. Śhrī Rāma accepted the sage's plea. Hearing about this, the fearful Gandharva went to Hanumān's mother, Añjanā. Crying out loud, he said, "Mother, my life is in great danger. Please save me. Give me your word." Añjanā's motherly heart could not refuse his request. She told Hanumān, "Son, I have given my word to save his life. Make my words true." Hanumān agreed. When Śhrī Rāma arrived to kill the Gandharva, Hanumān told the Gandharva to stand behind him and chant the Rāma-mantra. Hanumān stood there with palms folded in prayer, chanting the Rāma mantra. All the arrows Rāma shot at the Gandharva returned and fell as flowers at Rāma's feet. Not a single arrow harmed the Gandharva. Hanumān and the Gandharva continued to chant Rāma's name. At last, Hanumān humbly prayed to Śhrī Rāma, "If you allow him, the Gandharva is willing to beg the sage's pardon." Śhrī Rāma and the sage agreed, and the matter was settled. The Gandharva no longer had to fear for his life.

From this episode, we understand that even when the Lord arrived to punish, the devotee did not flinch. Hanumān did not try to compete with Rāma. Even as each arrow came in his direction, he closed his eyes and meditated upon his Lord. The Lord used this incident to reveal his devotee's greatness to the world. Hanumān did not try to convince Rāma to save the Gandharva who had taken refuge in him, nor did he ask the Lord for help. All he did was chant the Lord's name with utmost devotion and stand there. Hanumān had the firm faith that the Lord's will would never be detrimental to him. Hanumān never thought, "How could the Lord send arrows towards me, his devotee?" He was ready to accept the Lord's will, whatever it might be. This is the attitude of a true devotee. This is the ideal we should strive for.

Yet today, everyone wants to be a king or a manager. In such a situation, there will be only war. Everyone is intent on managing others, but if we can manage our own minds, we can always be the manager. By bringing the mind under our control, we can remain equipoised, regardless of what we hear, see, or the situations we face. We will stay anchored in our true self, and no one will be able to shake us from it. We will be able to witness every circumstance as if we are observing a game.

63

Question: What are the pañcha mahā yajñas?

Amma: Yajña is the principle by which people of any land and at any age, can learn to live with mutual love and cooperation by obeying the laws of nature. The pañcha mahā yajñas (the five great oblations) originated from the concept that we are duty-bound to give back a portion of what we take from nature.

The five great oblations that a householder should perform daily are: ṛiṣhi yajña – the study of spiritual texts; dēva yajña – pūjā (ritualistic worship), hōma (fire offerings), and other forms of worship of the divine; pitṛu yajña – protecting our parents, offering to ancestors to liberate their souls and seek their blessings; manuṣhya yajña – welcoming guests and attending to their needs; and bhūta yajña – protection of birds and animals.

The scriptural texts teach us how to live, reveal the nature of the world, and guide us on overcoming challenging situations in life without despair. Scriptures convey to us the principles underpinning our lives. When we read the scriptures daily, live faithful to their teachings and spread their message, we pay back our debt to the sages. This is ṛiṣhi yajña.

Dēva yajña involves worship of God and should become an integral part of daily life. Ritualistic worship, chanting the Lord's name, meditation, and observing fasting vows are all aspects of dēva yajña. Through such practices, the mind becomes focused and positive and the intellect becomes sharp and pure. By chanting mantras, we can stop other thoughts from entering the mind. Through meditation, our intelligence becomes luminous, and the vacillations of the mind subside, bringing peace and contentment. Performing pūjā and hōma, with a proper understanding of their foundational knowledge, is highly beneficial. When we offer oblations into the hōma fire, we should visualize burning away our attachments to the objects we like.

Pitṛu yajña is not merely the performance of tarpaṇa — offerings made to our forefathers. Pitṛu yajña becomes meaningful only when we show our respect and love to our parents and older people and serve them sincerely. If we do not properly care for our aged and bedridden parents, the pain in their hearts will remain in the atmosphere. Their deeply felt sorrow and laments, recorded in nature, will one day boomerang back to us. It is said that by sincerely caring for our parents, there is no need for any other forms of worship. We can repay at least a portion of our debt to the parents who nurtured and raised us by loving and serving them.

Our culture advises us to treat the guest as God — this is manuṣhya yajña. The love we have for our family members stems from our attachment to them, which will not help to make us broad-hearted. Treating guests with sacred regard, that is, serving the world, is based on love that has no expectations. It makes us fit to see the world as one family and to love and serve it. It leads us to expansiveness.

Trees and plants have been given the status of dēvatās — divine beings — and birds and animals are considered the vehicles of God. Bhūta yajña is respecting and consciously caring for them. In earlier times, people of the house would eat only after watering the basil, peepal, and bael trees and feeding the household animals. As we plant a flowering plant to propagate new flowers for worship, water it, watch the flowers bloom, and then pluck them and string a garland for God, our mind rests not on the actions but on God.

Nature endures great sacrifices for us. Look at the extent of the sacrifices made by rivers, animals, trees, etc. Look at a tree — it gives fruit, shade, and coolness. Even while being cut down, it continues to provide shade to the woodcutter.

Everything in nature makes great sacrifices for humanity. But what are we doing in return?

First and foremost, we must protect nature. Only then will we survive. We should abandon our habit of destroying nature for wealth and other selfish interests. The pañcha mahā yajñas help us with this.

64

Question: What is the need for spiritual texts?

Amma: The scriptures are the teachings of those who have seen the truth. They help us discriminate between right and wrong, travel on the right path, and fulfill our human birth. By learning the scriptures, the way to self-realization is easily cleared.

We should make an effort to grasp the essence of the scriptures and incorporate their teachings into our lives. Without this incorporation, scriptural study does not benefit us. We cannot reach the goal of God-realization solely by studying spiritual texts — the scriptures only point the way. For instance, a signboard was placed in a town directing the way to a famous gold shop. If we ask the signboard, we will not get any gold from it. If we want to buy gold ornaments, we must go to the shop. Similarly, scriptures are like those signboards; they point out the way. To reach the goal of God-realization, we must practice the prescribed spiritual disciplines.

The tree is contained within the seed. But for the seed to grow into a tree, keeping it in our hands is not enough; the seed has to be sown underneath the ground, and water and fertilizer must be provided for it. Likewise, what we are searching for is within us. But to realize this, we should assimilate and practice the spiritual principles expounded in the scriptures. The knowledge we gain through scriptural studies should be reflected in our thoughts, words, and actions. Spiritual practices should be performed following the guru's instructions. Interacting with those for whom knowledge has become a blissful experience will bring about a transformation in the lives of others.

Once, a guru called his disciples and said, "Come, let us go and teach spirituality to the people in town." They walked through the town streets, meeting many kinds of people. They spoke with some and smiled at others; they were loving toward the young children. As the day grew dark, one of the disciples asked the Guru, "Guru, it is getting late. When will we start our discourse?"

The guru said, "What have we been doing all this while? We have crossed paths with so many people, engaging with them and offering help in any little way we could. Those who interacted with us would have recognized the spiritual wealth within us. This recognition will inspire them to seek spiritual wealth within themselves. What greater spiritual message can we give them?"

Vedantic texts state that the moment a person gains self-knowledge, they will experience perfection and peace. However, if a disciple, despite learning the scriptures and listening to the guru's teachings, cannot experience this perfection, they should know that there are some obstacles within. The guru will guide the disciple on how to remove these obstacles. The process of attempting to remove these internal obstacles is called sādhanā — disciplined spiritual practice with the goal of liberation.

Even though we learn "*tat tvam asi* — You are *that*!" and "*aham brahmāsmi* — I am brahman," for the light of knowledge to shine through, the inner ignorance must vanish. Sādhanā is for this purpose. Until the ignorance within has been dispelled, proclaiming "*aham brahmāsmi*" is like naming a blind child "light" and calling them by that name.

If all the components to make a radio are correctly assembled, connected to a battery, and tuned, broadcasts from far-off radio stations will come into our homes for us to hear. Likewise, if we tune our minds through sādhanā, that is, if we assimilate and follow the words of scriptures and guru, we will experience the blissful self even while living in the physical body.

Through learning the scriptures, we should be able to remain peaceful and content, to love and honor all people, and to remain even-minded even in adverse circumstances. Scriptural study that does not bring about these changes is meaningless. We should overcome our tendency to wrongly interpret the scriptural statements and spiritual principles to cover up our failings and wrongdoing.

Once, a traveler was sitting and smoking a cigarette under the shade of a tree right in front of a temple dedicated to Dēvī. Seeing this, the priest commented, "Look, this is a sacred temple.

Please do not sit and smoke here." The traveler flew into a rage, "I am nobody's slave. I am my own boss. I do not like anyone trying to control me. I know well what can and what cannot be done. It is the same flame that shines in the lamp in front of Dēvī's statue that also shines at the tip of my cigarette. I see Dēvī in both. When this is the case, what is wrong with smoking here?"

Hearing this, the pūjārī said, "If you can see Dēvī everywhere and in everything, then you will not need to seek happiness from a cigarette. Today, you are enslaved by the cigarette. You still cannot assimilate the scriptural saying that one cannot find true happiness from an external object. The source of true joy is within ourselves. Also, one who sees God in all objects will never do something like this. They will always be, in all matters, an ideal model for others. Each word and action of such a person will inspire others to walk in the path of goodness. You are twisting the meaning of spiritual principles to hide and also to justify your failings and weaknesses. First, you need to recognize, accept, and overcome your failings and shortcomings. Only then can someone say, 'I am my own boss.'"

Likewise, we should discern the right meaning of the scriptures and live in the true spirit of their words, thus making our lives blessed.

65

Question: Is mastery of Sanskrit needed to live a spiritual life?

Amma: Sanskrit is our mother. It is the language of our culture; we cannot separate Sanskrit from our culture. It is not possible to correctly understand the *Vēdas*, *Upaniṣhads*, and *Bhagavad Gītā* without knowing Sanskrit. To understand the exact meaning of the mantras, we have to learn them in Sanskrit. We may say that we can get translations of the scriptures in many languages, but they are not sufficient — we can savor the sweetness of honey only if we taste it as pure honey. Researchers have found that speaking in Sanskrit and uttering Sanskrit terms enhances brain function.

Yet, we must be very aware of one thing: Learning Sanskrit should not be about showcasing our punditry. It should be to nourish our saṁskāra — our inner culture. It should be to understand our scriptures. Sanskrit should be seen as a means to attain these. Once we know from a newspaper where ripe mangoes are available, we should go to the shop, buy them, and eat them instead of sitting and looking at the picture in the paper. That is the intelligent action. It is good to know Sanskrit, but we do not need to spend our entire lives learning vyākaraṇam — the rules of grammar.

A man goes to the railway station. Once he has checked the timetable and discovered the time and ticket fare for the train to his destination, shouldn't he then purchase a ticket and board the train upon its arrival? Most so-called pundits are like those who spend their time learning the entire railway timetable by heart. They forget life's goal. There is a sack full of sugar: Do we need to eat the entire sack full of sugar to know whether it is sweet? When we are hungry, we should eat to satiate our hunger, but we need not eat all the items in the store. However, some people think differently; they want to eat all of it. Thus, their life is wasted.

It is good to learn Sanskrit to assimilate our culture in its entirety. The four *Vēdas* and the six systems of philosophy arose from within the great sages. In deep meditation, everything becomes clear. What a sage can learn in a day will take others ten days to master. Therefore, spiritual discipline and meditation are essential. We should understand Sanskrit and the scriptures, yet at the same time, we should remain aware of their real benefits. Our learning should be to know the goal of human life and the way to reach the goal. Once we know the goal and the way, we should make an effort to move forward on the path. We should live according to the spiritual principles. We will not reach anywhere through mere punditry.

Some people sit and read the *Bhagavad Gītā* and the *Upaniṣhads* in the temple grounds, but if someone walks near them, they get angry. Oblivious of the spiritual principles, they merely cling to customs. What kind of devotion is this? They repeat the spiritual principles someone uttered like a tape recorder. They are unable to emulate them in their lives. They do not know how to behave with love towards anyone. There is no moment when they are free of ego and jealousy. What is the benefit of such punditry? One must develop love towards fellow beings and compassion towards those who suffer. Otherwise, we will become selfish and self-centered and will not be able to experience God.

If you observe pundits today, you will see they have book knowledge but have never had any experience. Because of this lack, even though they studied until they were ninety, they have never been free of sorrow. They spend their lives just repeating what they have learned. Some sit idle at home.

Learn what is useful and then perform spiritual practices and meditation. If these are done, the knowledge gained will benefit both the world and oneself. Only through tapas (austerities) will we gain the experience we have read about. Only then will we attain peace. We should develop an attitude of offering the strength we gain through our austerities and spiritual disciplines to the world. We should make an effort to uplift those who suffer because they are unaware of the highest goal of life and the path to it. Through our sincere actions, many will benefit. We should be free of desire — only then will we attain perfection. Spirituality begins with compassion, and its perfection is also in compassion. We should not forget this.

66

Question: What is the importance of the *Bhagavad Gītā*?

Amma: The *Bhagavad Gītā* is the essence of all the *Vēdas*, which are as vast and deep as the ocean. Ordinary people cannot utilize ocean water to drink or for their needs around the house. But when the waters of the ocean evaporate in the sun's heat and form clouds, when the clouds rain down and flow as rivers, then humanity quenches its thirst and uses such water for many purposes. Likewise, with the grace of Lord Kṛishṇa, the *Vēdas* have flowed down to us in the form of this Ganga of spiritual wisdom.

The *Gītā's* message is for the entire human race. It expounds the paths to liberation through bhakti (devotion), jñāna (knowledge), and karma (action). The *Gītā* also expresses many spiritual principles and prescribes diverse forms of sādhanā (spiritual discipline). Lord Kṛishṇa came to show the way and guide people from various cultures to attain the highest reality. If a restaurant serves only one item, only those who like that particular food will come to eat there. Varieties of food with different tastes will attract everyone. If all clothes are stitched to the same measurement, they won't fit everyone. However, clothes tailored to different sizes benefit everyone. Likewise, the *Bhagavad Gītā* shows the way for people from all walks of life to reach the supreme goal of life — self-realization. The Lord's words will grasp our hands and elevate us from our current level of spiritual growth.

Some say that the *Bhagavad Gītā* encourages warfare. In reality, the *Gītā* shows individuals and society how to rise to peace. In situations where war is unavoidable, through the medium of the *Gītā*, Bhagavān teaches us how to make even such a battle into a spiritual practice. In the incident of Dakṣha's yajña, we see how Dakṣha's ego turned even a yajña — a sacred fire ritual — into war. Whereas Arjuna, accepting and following the Lord's teachings, fought his war as an offering to God, and turned his battle into a yajña — a ritual of sacrifice. The secret of karma (action) is the main message of the *Gītā*: how to transform karma into yōga — how to perform actions in a manner that unites us with God.

The *Gītā* does not contain sectarianism or narrow-mindedness. It does not ask us to worship a God living above the skies, seated on a golden throne, or to strive for a heaven that we gain after death. How do we experience the state of supreme peace here and now? The *Gītā* shows us the way. The *Gītā* illumines the path to realize the supreme truth, which resides as the Me in me.

Even though compact, the *Gītā's* message has the depth and vastness of the ocean. The *Gītā* stands as the symbol of Sanātana Dharma, and the *Gītā* will continue to bless the world as the Lord's eternal presence.

67

Question: The *Purāṇas* contain many stories and allusions that are illogical. What is their significance?

Amma: The Hindu religion considers the *Vēdas* to be the ultimate authority. If we doubt lines in a *Purāṇa*, we should look for corroboration in the *Vēdas*. The āchāryas (preceptors) have ruled that those lines that contradict the *Vēdas* should be rejected. The *Purāṇas* contain the knowledge of the *Vēdas* in the form of stories relevant to those times and were meant to inspire and uplift people. The spiritual principles embedded in the Puranic stories should be explored with the help of scriptural texts. If we get a piece of sugar cane, we will not chew and eat it all up. We savor the sweet juice and spit out the rind. We find many stories in the *Purāṇas* and some may not satisfy our logic. However, each one of them has been written with the intention of reaching people who are at different stages of spiritual and mental maturity. The ultimate goal of these stories is to reveal the one supreme truth.

The *Purāṇas* were written with the goal of awakening a taste for spirituality in people of different saṁskāras (cultural conditioning and mental refinement). When we read them, one part or the other will capture our mind and we will gain the insight needed to move forward in our life. The same incident is described differently for a small child, a youth, and an older adult, because it has to be described in such a way that they feel attracted to it and can enjoy it. Some may wonder why such detailed accounts were given for a particular incident, but only if told in such a manner will the person for whom it is intended understand the matter thoroughly. For this, we need to go to that individual's mental and spiritual level. A grown-up should not judge the mental level of a child from his own level. So, even though some of the stories of the *Purāṇas* seem far-fetched or made up, we will marvel at the foresight of the sages when we comprehend the level of those to whom they are revealing a particular principle.

In the *Purāṇas*, the sages give a very clear picture of future happenings. If we understand this, our respect for the *Purāṇas* will increase. We can learn this from reading how Kali Yuga (the present age of materialism and ignorance) is described in the *Bhāgavatam* (also known as *Bhāgavata Purāṇa*). The *Bhāgavatam* was composed many centuries ago, yet it describes many things that happen around us now. Although the scriptures do not consider the *Purāṇas* and *Smṛiti*[18] texts to be mukhya pramāṇa – the most authoritative source of knowledge – everything written in those books is unfolding precisely as described. All the stories in the *Purāṇas* have an inner meaning, which we should try to understand.

---

[18] Literally 'that which is remembered,' a class of sacred texts composed by ṛiṣhis. *Smṛiti*, denoting texts of human origin, is often contrasted with *Śhruti* ('that which is heard'), which refers to authoritative scriptural texts considered to be of divine origin.

68

Question: The scriptures tell us that God is within us and not separate from us. If this is so, what is the need for a guru?

Amma: True, God is within us. But to experience God, one needs help from a guru. To awaken someone from sleep, you need another who is awake. Likewise, the help of a self-realized guru who has spiritual and religious knowledge is needed to awaken all of us who are in the state of ajñāna – spiritual ignorance.

If we are given the first line of a poem we learned by heart in childhood but have since forgotten, we will immediately recall the rest of the lines. Similarly, we are currently in a state of forgetfulness, and the teachings of the guru have the power to awaken us from this state of forgetfulness.

The tree is contained within the seed, but it will grow and flourish only if the seed goes under the ground and its shell breaks. Likewise, even though we are the supreme truth, only when the shell of our ego breaks will we realize this truth. The guru is the one who creates the right circumstances for this. A small sapling needs a suitable climate to grow into a big tree. It needs water and fertilizer at the proper times and pests that attack it must be destroyed. In the same way, the guru creates a conducive environment for the disciples and protects them from all adversities.

The guru strives to eradicate the sense of "I" in the disciple. Obeying the guru's words is not slavery — it is the way to supreme freedom and eternal bliss. The guru has only one goal — the disciple's freedom from sorrow.

We are instructed to wear a seat belt when we sit in an airplane. This is not to deny us our freedom, but to protect us. Likewise, the guru advises the disciples to follow the yamas (regulations — the "don'ts"), niyamas (observances — the "dos"), and other disciplines for their spiritual growth and upliftment, and to save the disciple from dangers that may befall them.

A sculptor sees in his mind's eye the sculpture hidden in a stone. When he chisels away the unwanted parts of the stone, the sculpture reveals itself. Similarly, the guru reveals and illumines the divinity hidden within the disciple. When the disciple performs the sādhanā (spiritual disciplines) instructed by their guru, the disciple's ignorance is destroyed, and the truth within shines through. It can be compared to a sculpture covered in wax that is kept near a fire: when the wax melts, the sculpture reveals itself.

Guru is not merely an individual; guru is the supreme principle, the embodiment of ideals such as dharma, tyāga (renunciation), and prēma (supreme love). In the guru's presence, the disciple is able to assimilate these qualities and elevate themselves. This is the greatness of the guru's presence.

69

Question: Isn't spirituality and sannyāsa a desertion from life's responsibilities?

Amma: Spirituality is never an avoidance or desertion from life's responsibilities. It is the ability to understand the nature of the mind and the world — to know oneself — and thus to live with peace and contentment in any situation. Spirituality can be earned only through practice.

First, we need the right knowledge about the world and its objects. Our worldly attachments to people and objects will leave us when we gain this knowledge. Then even while living in society, we can perform our actions without attachment.

A bank manager handles money transactions worth millions of dollars every day and approves many loans. He is well aware that he is only a bank official and that the money he handles is not his own. He knows that the love and respect he shows those who come to deposit cash or take loans are only a part of his job. He is not particularly attached to the cash in the bank or to the people who make the deposits. Similarly, we should perform all our actions with the awareness that they are a responsibility that God has entrusted to us. Then each of our actions will become karma yōga – it will unite us with the Lord. It is not the actions that matter most, but rather the attitude with which we perform them.

Amma remembers a story: A householder disciple would always say to his guru, "O Guru, I am always in trouble. At home, I fight with my wife, and we always differ in our opinions. At the office, not a day goes by without my superior officer scolding me. He has even stopped my pay raises many times. I cannot sleep because of the tension that all this causes me." Even though the guru spent a lot of time and effort advising the disciple, it was to no avail; the disciple was unable to imbibe his teachings.

One day, at the same time that the disciple would come to visit every day, the guru went and tightly hugged a thorny tree that grew in front of the ashram. Then he started crying out, "Save me, save me, someone come and save me! The thorns are piercing my body, the thorns are piercing me!" Hearing the guru's loud cries, the disciple ran up to the tree, saw what was happening and asked, "What foolishness is this? What are you talking about? You are the one hugging the tree. Why don't you just let go?" Pretending not to hear his words, the guru continued to cry out, "Someone come and save me." Then the disciple said, "What are you saying? How can this tree catch hold of you? Let go of the tree, then you will have no more pain." The guru immediately let go of the thorny tree and said, "This is exactly what you are doing. You are the one holding onto your troubles. Without your permission, how is it possible for them to enter your mind? I have repeated this to you many times, but you did not understand or were not ready to accept my words. Like the tree that cannot hold on to us, no objects in this world can bind us or bring sorrow to us. On the contrary, we bind ourselves to them. The very moment our attachment to them vanishes, we will become free of bondage."

If a man attending a festival knows that loud fireworks will go off at any moment, he will not be scared but rather enjoy the loud bangs. A man who is entirely unaware of this will be badly shaken when he hears them. Likewise, if we know the nature of the world, we will not falter, whatever circumstances we may face. Spirituality is the right knowledge about ourselves and the world. If we have this knowledge, we will never be defeated by life and we will never allow depression to overpower us.

Each and every relationship and object of the world are subject to change. What keeps changing can never give us eternal peace. Knowing this truth, we must offer ourselves to God. Then no sorrow will touch us. We will be able to live contentedly in this world, accepting both honor and dishonor, success and failure, joy and sorrow with an even mind. Scriptural science shows us the way to attain this state.

70

Question: Is knowledge of spirituality necessary to serve people?

Amma: Many people are actively working for one political party or another. They became attracted to these parties after observing the lives led by the party leaders, their sacrifices, their idealism, and so on. They work for the party, adopting the leader's principles. Amma says it is better to embrace spiritual principles, because revenge, selfishness, or hatred are not embedded in them. Can you find an ideal anywhere that is superior to what is set forth in the *Bhagavad Gītā*?

If one has a heart that sincerely thinks of performing actions that benefit the world instead of singing devotional songs, chanting the name of God, or praying, that is enough. Because God is not someone who lives above the sky – he is all-pervading. The creator and his creation are not two. Gold and ornaments made of gold are not two – the chain is implicit in the gold, and gold is what the chain is made of. We are in God – God is in us. It is ideal to see God in humanity and to serve the people, but such a bhāva (attitude) should be there in its totality. Performing actions with one hundred percent detachment is very difficult. Selfishness will creep in unknowingly. Then we will not get the perfect fruits of selfless action.

People say that we need equality, there should be no distinction between workers and employers. But how many employers would like to give up their post to a worker and have them sit in their chair? How many political leaders who assert the worker's rights will give up their own position to a follower? It is not enough to proclaim selflessness; it should be revealed in actions. This will not happen all of a sudden in a single day. Constant spiritual practice is needed to develop this quality. We should be careful that only good thoughts accompany each of our breaths. We should try to develop good qualities in our mind. The breath of such people will spread good vibrations in the atmosphere. We hear people say that factories pollute the atmosphere, but man's mind holds an even deadlier poison — the ego. We should fear this ego more than anything else. An egoic mind can be purified with the help of devotional singing, prayer, and other spiritual practices.

If we channel water that flows in different directions into one powerful stream, we can generate electricity from it. In a similar way, japa (chanting the holy name) and meditation can take control of our mental energy which is otherwise frittered away in many thoughts. By such control, the mind's energy is conserved and will not be drained away. If an ordinary human is like an electric pole, the tapasvī (a performer of spiritual austerity) can be compared to a transformer.

A laborer who carried loads on his head for a living educated himself and became a scientist. The same head that once bore heavy loads now became a scientist's. But can the intellectual capabilities of a scientist be compared to that of a laborer carrying loads on his head? If a laborer can become a scientist, why can't an ordinary human grow to the expansiveness of a spiritual being? It is possible through spiritual practices, a selfless attitude, and good thoughts. With single-minded focus, the strength of the mind can be greatly increased and conserved. The power gained through mantra japa can be used to benefit the world. There is no selfishness in such actions. Only good words and good actions will flow to the world from such people. Every spiritual practice is intended for gaining a mind that allows us to offer ourselves to the world. Yet,

Amma is willing to perform pāda pūjā[19] to those who offer their lives to the world even without performing any of these spiritual practices. The fruits of prayer can equally be gained through selfless service. When selflessness dawns, the individual vanishes.

Through meditation and other spiritual practices, the mind will gain the capacity to adjust to various circumstances. Nowadays people always carry a lot of tension. Japa is the practice to get rid of tension. Children need mañchāḍi kurus (red lucky seeds) when they first learn to count. Using these seeds, we teach them to count one, two, etc. Later on, even without the red lucky seeds, they learn mental calculation. A forgetful person will take a list of things to be purchased with him when he goes shopping. Once he has bought those items, the list can be discarded. Likewise, today we are in a state of forgetfulness, not wakefulness. Until we achieve wakefulness, we need to perform japa and other spiritual practices. Once the mind has lost its selfishness through spiritual practices, sēvā (selfless service)

---

[19] Ceremonial washing of the feet as a form of worship.

also becomes a sādhanā for realizing the highest goal of liberation.

When we paste the notice "Do not stick advertisements" on a wall, we can prevent other notices from being pasted there. Even "Do not stick advertisements" is a notice, but it is of great benefit. Mantra japa is similar to this. Through mantra japa, we can reduce the number of thoughts in our mind. Other thoughts do not enter the mind during the time we spend repeating the mantra. Through this, we become free of the tension created by thoughts; the mind becomes pure. There is no hostility or thoughts of revenge, and the mind becomes peaceful, at least for the time spent in mantra repetition. Japa creates good vibrations in the atmosphere. The mind becomes less selfish and more generous and service comes naturally to such a mind. The stress and conflicts within our mind will not vanish just because we serve humanity — spiritual practices are also needed for a calm mind. Then we can serve without any complaints or feelings of humiliation; we will be able to serve with joy.

In our country and in the entire world, countless people suffer from poverty and ignorance. We must do everything we can to end their suffering and share the light of knowledge with them. There is no greater religion or science than encouraging someone who has lost hope or helping someone who is suffering. A life dedicated to service is blessed. Such sēvaks (selfless servants) are the cornerstones of our culture. Selfless service has an unparalleled power to transform and inspire.

The root cause of society's problems today is ignorance about our saṁskāra – our culture and traditions – and the principles on which it is founded. Ignorance, disunity, and indolence – these three are our curses. Through enthusiastic and inspired action, we should overcome all three. We also need a system of education that gives us knowledge of our own culture and the strength to stand on our own feet. We are indebted to this earth and to this culture that has nurtured us and made us what we are. This earth is our mother. Ārṣhasaṁskṛiti – the culture established by the ṛiṣhis – is our mother. We should fulfill our obligations to her.

71

Question: Why has nature lost its rhythm to such a great extent? What solution does our culture have for nature's loss of rhythm and harmony?

Amma: When man abandons dharma, nature loses its harmony and rhythm. We should become a culture that gives instead of a culture that takes – giving is the dharma of nature. Yet humans, due to their selfishness, have forgotten their dharma of giving. The hardships we experience now are the result of this forgetfulness. When agriculture becomes just a way to make money, it will destroy the balance of nature. Agriculture is a means for humanity to produce food; its aim should not be to amass wealth. Food is meant not just for humans but also for birds and animals. We get the harvest only if we sow the seeds; through this action, we should know that we gain when we give. When agriculture becomes a means to make money, selfish people will not hesitate to exploit nature in many ways. This leads to the death of thousands of living beings – both plant and animal – and eventually, it will pave the way for man's extinction. Can humanity survive independently without relying on birds, animals, trees, and plants? The cataracts of selfishness have blinded today's generation; they are unable to see this truth.

When we forsake dharma, climate changes will occur. Weather patterns will shift; we will not get rain on time, and droughts will last longer. As science has predicted, hunger will increase.

Humanity is part of nature. Our prana (vital energy) is inextricably intertwined with birds, trees, animals, and all other living beings. A healthy life becomes possible when our lifestyle harmonizes with the lives of other beings. All beings in nature exist in mutual interdependence. Trees take water and nutrients out of the soil through their roots; their leaves and fruits become food with the help of sunlight and air. Humans, birds, and animals receive food from these plants and trees. Trees are necessary to purify the air we live in. Humanity survives because plants, trees, birds, and animals exist in nature. If they cease to exist, humanity also ends and there will be no civilization. If we consider nature as one vast tree, we can say that its roots, branches, leaves, flowers, and fruits are the totality of living beings. This tree will attain perfection only when that totality functions harmoniously. When even one plant or animal species becomes extinct, its loss can be felt in the entire ecosystem. Although we may not immediately understand or feel the impact of the loss, we will eventually have to experience the after-effects. This universe is in a state of equilibrium, a balance in which everything sentient and insentient has its place — humanity must not upset this equilibrium, this harmony in nature. The well-being and survival of all creatures in nature is essential for the well-being and survival of humanity.

We cannot live without water, but we should not be inundated by it; floods will destroy everything. We cannot live without the wind, but we will lose our lives if it becomes a tornado. We need the earth to live upon, but if the earth shakes, that is the end of everything. Everything in this universe is needed for our existence, but everything should be in the right proportion; there should neither be too much nor too little. Nature should maintain this harmonious balance, and for this humanity needs to make the right efforts. To maintain nature's balance, we should know what dharma and adharma are, and live in dharma. We should be able to love and serve all. If we need to retain the harmony and balance of nature, we should learn to live with awareness of dharma, without killing animals or chopping down trees indiscriminately. If we do so, nature will reward us with good fruits for our actions.

Our ancestors told us to pray to God, the first cause of all this. Through such prayer, our individuality vanishes and we become one with the universe. We are able to tune in to the rhythm of the universe and live in harmony with it. Each component of the universe around us – birds, animals, trees, plants, and all of us – moves with the same rhythm. In this way, we are elevated to the realm of oneness. The bliss we then experience cannot be described in words. The way to reach this goal is to see everything as God and to love and serve – this is Sanātana Dharma.

We cannot stop floods or tornadoes from happening, and we cannot stop the earth from shaking. However, humanity's crimes can be stopped if we so desire. We can live discerning between dharma and adharma. If we really want to, we can end poverty; we only need to share with each other.

Everything will move in its own rhythm if we move forward in mutual love. Selfishness is not present if we only take what is necessary. Cutting down a branch when we need only a leaf is selfish — it is adharma. When we amass wealth not just for ourselves or our children, but for the next ten generations, it is adharma. Through such behavior, many others remain without food — this is a sin. Such a person cannot enjoy real happiness in their life because they are adharmic. This is why our ancestors told us to live with the knowledge of what dharma and adharma are. Their love for each other and each aspect of creation grew into worship. Loving, serving, and adoring all happened naturally — it was a natural progression, and no one needed exceptional motivation.

When the dark clouds of selfishness vacate the skies of our hearts, God's consciousness, akin to the sun, will shine constantly within. In that light, we will be able to see ourselves in everything around us. The darkness that had enveloped us until now will leave us forever. For one who is established in this constant experience of oneness, the worm that crawls in front of one's eyes, the bird, the elephant that shakes the forest, the buzzing mosquito, the eagle soaring high, the little fish and the crocodile, and man walking with his head held high, are all God. When we understand this truth, love will awaken within for all living beings around us, both sentient and insentient; our hearts will become expansive and all-inclusive. When love dawns, we will speak not only to humans but to birds, animals, rivers, and mountains. We will be able to talk to a little flower, the sky, and the Moon. When love fills our hearts, we will see life pulsating in everyone and everything around us — we will not even want to step on the earth as the thought will arise that it might hurt the earth. We will understand the hearts of birds and animals — love does not have any particular language. It speaks the language of the heart.

When we love all beings, our hearts become expansive — we will directly experience the divine consciousness pervading and illumining everything. We will see God's image in everything around us. Then affection will become love, and love will grow into worship. We will not be able to see anything as separate from us. Our ancestors said, "sarvaṁ brahmamayaṁ — there is nothing other than brahman in this entire universe," because they realized this blissful experience.

This vision is the cornerstone of our culture, the cornerstone of the Hindu religion. This is why loving all beings in creation is given such importance. Our mantra is, "lōkāḥ samastāḥ sukhinō bhavantu – may all beings in all the worlds be happy." We have not left anyone out in this mantra. The āchāryas of the Hindu religion did not have any hesitation in praying even for the well-being of deadly snakes whose single bite can kill. They knew the snake was alive, just like them, and within its heart resided the very same divine consciousness that resided in their hearts; hence, its life was also as valuable as theirs. Along with this awareness, they also realized the importance of every creature in maintaining nature's equilibrium. This is why our ancestors decreed sacred groves and specific rituals as part of our spiritual tradition to protect snakes and other creatures, trees, vines, and birds. In the sacred groves, *nūrum pālum* is a special oblation made with rice, turmeric, and cow's milk, which is offered as food for snakes. They lit stone lamps inside the sacred groves and, using unique beats and tunes, sang devotional songs to worship the trees and other living creatures. In Bhārat, sacred groves and ponds were a part of people's culture and social life.

However, selfishness has robbed humanity of this awareness of the oneness of all beings. Today, man lives in his own world created by his own mind, and suffers the consequences. Imperfection is not God's creation; it is humanity's creation. When we look with minds clouded by the ignorance of selfishness, we cannot see or experience the abundance of peace and beauty surrounding us.

Today, people often view everything around them as mere objects for their own selfish purposes. For them, birds, animals, trees, and other living beings are merely seen as food and tools to satiate their cravings for pleasure and a luxurious lifestyle. We have lost the capacity to see them as kin to our own selves. Our human lives will attain perfection only when we are able to see everything as ourselves. Only then will peace and contentment fill our lives. The sages who saw the truth envisaged this path for humanity to attain perfection: see all beings as God and love and serve. Only by following this path can we maintain the rhythm and harmony of nature.

72

Question: What is the attitude of the Hindu religion towards those who follow other religions?

Amma: The Hindu religion is not against anyone. It does not ask anyone to abandon their own religion or faith. In fact, the Hindu religion considers it adharma to destroy another person's beliefs. It views all religions as different paths to reach God and does not reject anything; it is inclusive of all. In short, the Hindu religion holds no hostility towards any other religion. Bhārat has never even had such a concept. Followers of any religion can stand firm in their faith and move forward. Being faithful to their own religion will help them reach the goal.

Those who belong to any religion will find that karma yōga, bhakti yōga, and jñāna yōga are suitable for these times and are compatible with their lifestyle. These practices are accessible to everyone. The ocean and its waves may terrify someone who cannot swim, but for those who know how to swim, the waves bring joy. In the same way, life becomes a celebration for those who have assimilated spirituality into their life. We need a way by which we can experience bliss not after death, but even while alive. Just as we need to learn business management to do business, we need to learn life management to fill our lives with contentment. Sanātana Dharma is the comprehensive science of life management.

The *Upanishads, Bhagavad Gītā, Brahma Sūtras, Rāmāyaṇa*, and *Mahābhārata* contain eternal truths that humanity should imbibe at all times. They are never divisive or sectarian. On the contrary, they are books based on logical inferences and analysis. These scriptures are practical guides to life that can benefit everyone. Like health sciences, psychology, and social sciences, the teachings of Sanātana Dharma can be accepted and understood universally. They do not persuade anyone to believe in one particular God or holy book. The Hindu religion has an all-inclusive and expansive vision.

Right from the time of our ancestors, people practicing religions from other parts of the world were free to live and worship in Bhārat. The proof of this can be seen in the diversity of religions and spiritual traditions that are followed here even today. Sanātana Dharma shows the entire human race the way to eternal peace.

73

Question: Don't some people allege that the dēvatās (deities) of the Hindu religion are demons?

Amma: This is because some people assert, "Only my religion is right, and yours is wrong." Such an approach inevitably leads to conflicts and clashes. Everyone should be careful not to speak this way. Some people may dismiss the speaker as irrational and tolerate it when they hear, "My mother is good, while yours is a prostitute." However, not all children will suffer in silence. Can you blame them for reacting to such an insult?

Love each other; do not sow the seeds of destruction. There is only one truth, and everyone should awaken to that truth. Learn your own religion well, and try to live according to its good and noble principles. We are all children of one mother. Love and respect each other, and thus become worthy of receiving God's grace.

Do not fight in the name of religion or become terrorists; instead, love one another. Help each other. Live in peace. This is what we need.

Some people criticize the diverse forms of Hindu worship as primitive, but such criticism stems from ignorance. If we understand them correctly, we will realize that the various deities and the rituals with which they are worshiped are rooted in high principles, ideals, and aims.

In the West, many homes have paintings displayed on the walls. Amma saw one such painting in a home she visited. An ordinary person wouldn't understand what it was — there were just five or six lines painted in four or five colors; that was all. It looked as if a broom had been dipped in paint and spread across the canvas. Yet, this painting was worth five million dollars. Security had been hired to protect it from theft, and security cameras had been installed. We didn't understand anything about it, but the owner could speak for hours about the painting. No one would say that the painter was an idiot; on the contrary, they were hailed as a great artist. "So many people are starving; why did you spend so much money on such a painting?" — no one would ask the buyer such a question. The painting's value doesn't diminish just because the ordinary person doesn't know the meaning of those lines. Likewise, we will appreciate the greatness and significance of the dēvatās in the

Hindu religion only when the high principles behind their conception are understood.

The real wealth of Bhārat lies in its culture. Yet, we do not strive to understand it. Our faith has become confined to traditional observances and festivals, and is so weak that it will collapse at even the slightest criticism. Therefore, we must be willing to understand the foundational knowledge of our culture as revealed in the scriptures and assimilate it into our lives.

From the perspective of Sanātana Dharma, God is the all-pervading divine consciousness that transcends all names, forms, and qualities. The various qualities of God shine through the forms of the Dēvīs and Dēvas (goddesses and gods). Hanumān represents the principle of conquering the mind, which is as fickle and capricious as a monkey. Praṇava is the ādināda – the first sound (Ōm), the primordial sacred sound that contains the essence of the absolute. Gaṇapati (Gaṇēśha) is the personification of praṇava, which is why he is worshiped first.

Each form of a deity embodies many subtle meanings. We may worship the forms of any of the gods and goddesses, but ultimately, we reach the supreme self, the formless absolute reality.

74

Question: What are Amma's views on religious conversion?

Amma: It should be one's own decision to convert from one religion to another. Amma will not say whether it is right or wrong. Amma would never tell anyone to change their religion. It is enough to know yourself. It is saddening when people are unable to discover who they truly are.

Amma gives Christ's mantra to the Christians and other suitable mantras to her Muslim children. Whatever religion you believe in, if you have the qualities of love, compassion, and kindness in your life, Amma says that you will be able to experience peace. There is no need to change one's religion for this.

It is incredibly impractical to insist that everyone in the world should wear the same size shoes, wear clothes that are all the same size and fashion, and eat the same food. It is equally impractical to say that everyone should follow only one guru, one prophet, one holy book. Children, women, and men wear clothes and shoes in the sizes and fashions suited to the climate and circumstances in which they live. Once we choose a path, we should remain committed to it. Those who follow many paths reach nowhere. However, whichever path you follow should be chosen only after proper reflection.

Religions are man's creation. God has not created any particular religion. Rāma, Kṛiṣhṇa, and Christ did not create religions. At different times and in different places, teachers come to uplift people who have different temperaments. Religions were created later on by followers who had imbibed their teachings.

Because of diverse cultures and differences in people's inclinations, it became necessary to create many different religions. While each has its own relevance, no single religion is universally suitable for all human beings. If people understood this truth, they would realize how illogical their thoughts on religious conversion are, and would no longer want to convert others to their religion.

Spirituality is the innermost core of religion, while beliefs and religious observances are only the rind, the outer skin. Spirituality means awakening to one's own self. The true religious believer is one who awakens to his own self. The more we awaken to the true essence within ourselves, the more we become free from the constraints imposed by the framework of religion. When one knows oneself perfectly, one realizes that there is only one truth, and nothing in this universe is separate from oneself. All differences, all divisive thoughts, and all fears end.

Amma remembers a story: A circus company's tiger died, and even though the manager searched far and wide, he could not find a new one. Then one day, a man came searching for a job, but the circus manager told him, "We have enough people; we don't need anyone presently." The man begged for a job, so the manager said, "OK, we have one vacancy. Our tiger died. Can you dress up as a tiger in his stead?" Needing money, the man agreed to dress up as a tiger. He put on a tiger skin and was trained to walk and behave like a tiger. He was paraded on a leash when the show started, and then he was tied up inside a cage. One day, the tiger was tied up close to the circus lion in the same cage. The man-tiger suddenly noticed the lion standing nearby, tied up with a rope as flimsy as his own. If the lion broke free from his rope, the man-tiger's demise was assured.

The lion was watching the man-tiger narrowly as he walked around inside the cage. The man's heart started beating very fast. The lion had stopped walking and was carefully observing the tiger as if ready to pounce on him. The man-tiger thought, "At any moment, he will pounce on me! So, before I become lion food, let me pray. Only God can save me now." The man dressed up as a tiger closed his eyes, lay down on the floor and started praying with folded palms. He was waiting for the moment when the lion would pounce on him. Despite praying, his dread was increasing. Even while lying face-down, he continued to watch the lion's movements out of the corner of his eye. After a while, he could no longer hear the sound of the lion's padded paws. Was he getting ready to pounce? He looked again at the lion out of the corner of his eye and was amazed.

The lion, too, was lying face-down on the floor of the cage, watching him out of the corner of his eye. His posture and demeanor were not that of a lion; they seemed more like that of a man. As he looked more carefully and saw the lion watching him, he suddenly understood that this too was not a real lion, but a man dressed in a lion skin, just as he was dressed in his tiger skin. At that moment, the lion also understood the truth, and they both ran towards each other and hugged. They had been scared to death of each other, wondering who would pounce first, but fear left them the moment they understood who they both really were. They embraced each other with love as they were overwhelmed by the joy of escaping death.

Both of them only gained this knowledge when they surrendered to God and bowed down before Him. We will recognize our true form, our real nature, only through surrender and humility. Once our preconceptions and prejudgements of others vanish, we will see that they are not separate from us — and then, all fear will leave us. At our core, we are all the same; our core is peace and love. Fundamentally, we are one; there is no need for fear, hatred, or jealousy. Differences are only at the surface level. There is no divisiveness where there is the blissful experience of the truth. Wherever there is divisiveness, there is no experience of the blissful truth. When one starts awakening to one's own self, one becomes liberated from the binding ties of religion. Remaining bound by religious ties is like reaching the other shore on a ferry and remaining seated inside the boat, holding onto it, without stepping out onto the other shore. The boat is only an instrument, a vehicle to reach the other shore. Likewise, religion and all its traditions and observances are only instruments to reach God. We should not remain attached to religion forever. When someone points to a fruit hanging on a tree, we should not look at the finger, but look at the fruit.

We must understand the essence of all religions, but first, we need to know about the religion we were born into and raised in. We should understand the nature of spirituality. When we understand spirituality, we will not give undue importance to the framework within which religion functions. We should give importance not to increasing the number of members but to assimilating into our lives the qualities of truthfulness, dharma, compassion, love, kindness, non-violence, renunciation, etc., that religion espouses. It is not the number of believers that is important; what is important are the values and goodness that the believers possess. It is a great sin to destroy someone's faith; it is equal to murder. Once we have destroyed someone's faith, it is extremely difficult for that void to be filled again.

Religions began as paths to the supreme truth, but later, they became organizations. Then protecting the organizations' vested interests became more important than imbibing the noble qualities espoused by religion. An organization has its own rules, disciplines, beliefs, and traditions. Some people used these as instruments to maintain their authority and leadership. They interpreted spiritual principles according to their own interests. Often, they tried to impose their religion on others. Propagating their religion and converting others were used to increase these religious leaders' authority and influence.

Thus, we see religions that were originally born to lead humanity to ultimate freedom, are now binding humanity with the chains of religion. Religions that should spread peace and well-being in the world themselves became the reason for wars and discord. This should change. Whatever your faith, learn to grow from there itself, and allow others to do so as well. This is the way of dharma. We should understand that others also have expectations from the world that are similar to ours. We should know that we are all children of one mother. Then we will be able to relinquish mutual hostility. We will be able to forget all animosity and embrace each other. We should try to discover the heart of religions and step into a new era of love, oneness, and mutual respect.

75

Question: Why do we say that Sanātana Dharma is the most sublime and ancient?

Amma: Sanātana Dharma, also known as the Hindu religion, existed in this world long before the other major religions were born. When the new religions started spreading, the intrinsic culture and religion of each land and its people were lost. However, Sanātana Dharma overcame all challenges and continues to exist. The majority of the people of Bhārat continue to follow Sanātana Dharma, having prevailed over foreign invasions, centuries of foreign rule, and religious conversions.

Sanātana Dharma teaches us that God resides not only in human beings but in all creation, and that the one self inhabits all. This vision of equality, of the oneness of all, is unique to

Sanātana Dharma. God is the indivisible pure consciousness, the foundation of this constantly changing world. This world is not separate from God. Sanātana Dharma declares that creation and the creator are not two, but one. From this vision of oneness arose compassion towards all living beings. As everything in creation is a different facet of the one truth, our culture taught us to honor and worship even the tiniest creature. When the left-hand feels pain, the right-hand caresses it because both belong to the same body. Likewise, Sanātana Dharma teaches us to feel the pain of others as our pain, see their joy as our joy, and to love and serve them.

Sanātana Dharma believes in the law of karma. The results of our actions will return to us. Our good actions will bring joyful experiences, while our wrong actions will be the cause of pain and sorrow. Whether good or bad, the fruits of karma — our actions — are limited, and therefore, Sanātana Dharma does not have the concept of an eternal heaven or an eternal hell. For those who have done wrong, there are always opportunities to correct their mistakes and reform themselves. This is why God gives us new lives repeatedly.

Sanātana Dharma recognizes punarjanma (rebirth). When the jīva (individual self) realizes or attains union with God, it is liberated from the karma-chakra (the wheel of actions and their consequences), bringing an end to saṁsāra (the cycle of death and rebirth). In that state, there is the blissful experience of oneness with God. Anyone can gain this blissful experience, even while they are alive. In truth, we are all of the nature of God. We only need to drop the false identification with the body to attain the blissful experience of the self or God. In this, there is no distinction between nobleman and peasant, man or woman. This vision of advaita (non-duality) is unique to Sanātana Dharma. For those who have realized God, their true self, the world becomes a part of themselves. The world is one family. This is the all-inclusive, expansive view of Sanātana Dharma. It exhorts us to demonstrate kindness, compassion, and non-violence towards all beings. Sanātana Dharma does not see anyone as separate or alien.

God resides in all beings — both sentient and insentient. Sanātana Dharma proclaims that nature is a manifestation of God. This is why those who follow Sanātana Dharma honor and worship mountains, forests, rivers, oceans, trees, and even snakes, rats, and lizards as representations of the divine.

Dharma and yajña are the two main pillars of Sanātana Dharma. Dharma maintains and stabilizes the rhythm and harmony of this universe. Each of us must perform our own dharma — our ethical duties and responsibilities — so as not to disrupt this universal rhythm. We must not act in an adharmic manner; there should be no action on our part which harms other beings or disturbs the harmony of this universe.

Yajña means that all beings should move forward, nourishing and nurturing one another for the sake of the universal good. All unified actions for the welfare of creation are yajña. Sanātana Dharma calls upon us to perform all actions in the spirit of yajña.

Though Hindu dharma is firmly rooted in eternal truths, it tells us to accept the changes appropriate for the times. This is how the *Smṛitis* (texts attributed to ṛiṣhis, offering practical guidance relevant to specific times and places) were formulated. The hallmark of Sanātana Dharma is its expansive vision that incorporates everything, including the infallible reasoning and proof laid down in its scriptural texts.

Another unique feature of the Hindu religion is that it reaches out to people of different levels of spiritual and mental maturity, uplifting them from where they are. This is how the various paths of spiritual practice, such as jñāna yōga and bhakti yōga, were developed. People from all walks of life can elevate themselves through these paths.

Sanātana Dharma aims for the well-being and prosperity of the entire world. Its worldview is encapsulated in the phrase "*vasudhaiva kuṭumbakam* – the word is one family." Sanātana Dharma's message is the thread of oneness that strings together all beings in the universe.

ōm śhāntiḥ śhāntiḥ śhāntiḥ
Let there be peace, peace, and peace.

Glossary

abhayamudrā: sacred hand gesture (*mudrā*) that symbolizes protection and bestows fearlessness.

āchāra: traditional custom or observance; conduct.

āchārya: a spiritual guide or teacher, one who consolidates the essentials of the scriptures, establishes them in tradition, and observes them in practice.

adharma: unrighteousness; deviation from natural harmony.

adharmic: unrighteous.

ādiguru : the original or first guru, considered the source of all spiritual lineages and teachings; the one with whom the tradition of guru-disciple relationship began.

advaita: 'not two;' non-dual philosophy that holds that the *jīva* (individual soul) and *jagat* (universe) are essentially one with *brahman*, the supreme reality.

ahaṅkāra-buddhi: the aspect of intellect characterized by egoism and self-centeredness, where decisions and judgments are influenced by one's sense of identity and personal ego.

ajñāna: ignorance (of the spiritual truth); an *ajñānī* is one who is ignorant.

Amāvāsyā: the night of the new moon, first day of the lunar month.

anāchāras: improper actions that are not based on the principal teachings.

aṇḍa: egg.

Añjanā: mother of Hanumān.

ārādhanā: adoration of the divine.

Arjuna: great archer and one of the heroes of the *Mahābhārata*. It is Arjuna whom Kṛiṣhṇa addresses in the *Bhagavad Gītā*.

artha: goal; wealth; substance. One of the four *puruṣhārthas* (goals of human endeavor).

āśhram (ashram): 'place of striving.' A place where spiritual seekers and aspirants live or visit, in order to lead a spiritual life. It is usually the home of a spiritual master, saint or ascetic, who guides the aspirants.

āśhrama: one of the traditional four stages of life, beginning with *brahmacharya* (celibate student life), followed by *gārhasthya* (married householder life), *vānaprastha* (retired life dedicated to spiritual practices) and *sannyāsa* (complete renunciation of worldly affairs).

asura: demon, often (though not always) depicted as evil and antagonistic towards the *dēvas* (gods).

asuric: demonic.

ātmā-chaitanya: pure consciousness or self-awareness, representing the essential, unchanging nature of the self beyond individual identity and ego.

ātmā-kṛipā: grace of one's own self.

ātmā (ātman): the true self. The essential nature of our real existence. One of the fundamental tenets of *Sanātana Dharma* is that we are not the physical body, feelings, mind, intellect, or personality. We are the eternal, pure, unblemished self.

ātmānanda: bliss of the self.

avadhūta: an enlightened person whose behavior is often eccentric and at odds with social norms.

Ayōdhyā: ancient city; birthplace and kingdom of Lord Rāma.

bali: sacrificial offering.

bhaga: the six blessed qualities, viz. *jñāna* (knowledge), *aiśhvarya* (sovereignty), *śhakti* (energy), *bala* (might), *vīrya* (valor) and *tējas* (spiritual splendor). One who has all these qualities is known as *bhagavān* (God) or *bhagavatī* (Goddess).

Bhagavad Gītā: 'Song of the Lord,' it consists of 18 chapters of verses in which Lord Kṛiṣhṇa advises Arjuna. The advice is given on the battlefield of Kurukṣhētra, just before the righteous Pāṇḍavas fight the unrighteous Kauravas. It is a practical guide to overcoming crises in one's personal or social life and is the essence of Vedic wisdom.

Bhagavān: God, one who has all the six divine qualities pertaining to *bhaga* (see *bhaga*).

Bhāgavata Purāṇa: also known as *Bhāgavatam*, one of the eighteen *Purāṇas,* a devotional Sanskrit composition narrating the life, pastimes, and teachings of various incarnations of Viṣhṇu, chiefly that of Lord Kṛiṣhṇa.

Bhāgavatam: see *Bhāgavata Purāṇa.*

bhakti: devotion for God.

bhakti yōga: the path of devotion.

bhāva: divine mood or attitude.

Brahmā: Lord of Creation in the trinity of Brahmā, Viṣhṇu (Lord of Preservation), and Śhiva (Lord of Destruction).

brahmacharya: celibacy; one of the four stages of life (see āśhrama). *Brahma* also means *Vēda.* So, *brahmacharya* is the stage of life in which one pursues the study of the *Vēdas* with self-discipline under the guidance of a qualified teacher.

brahman: the absolute reality, supreme being; the whole; that which encompasses and pervades everything, and is one and indivisible.

brahmāṇḍa: universe, lit. 'cosmic egg.'

Brahmasthānam: 'abode of *brahman.*' The name of the temples Amma consecrated in various parts of India and in Mauritius. The temple shrine features a unique four-faced idol that symbolizes the unity behind the diversity of divine forms.

chitta-chōra: 'thief of the mind' or 'stealer of hearts,' an endearing name of Kṛiṣhṇa.

Dakṣha: father of Satī, the consort of Lord Śhiva. Once, Dakṣha insulted Lord Śhiva by not inviting him to his grand *yajña* (fire ritual), causing the humiliated and grief stricken Satī to voluntarily immolate herself in the flames of the sacrificial fire. This incident unleashed Śhiva's wrath. He killed Dakṣha and the *yajña* was completely destroyed. Dakṣha was later forgiven and revived.

darśhan: audience with a holy person or a vision of the divine. Amma's signature *darśhan* is a hug.

darśhana: philosophical system.

dāsya-bhakti: a form of devotion to God wherein the devotee embraces the role of a loyal and obedient servant.

dēva: deity or demi-god; divine being; celestial being. *Dēva* is the masculine form. The feminine equivalent is *dēvī*.

dēvalōka: abode of the *dēvas* (demi-gods).

Dēvī: goddess; Divine Mother.

Durgā: a fierce manifestation of the Divine Mother, often depicted as wielding a number of weapons and riding a lion or tiger.

Duryōdhana: eldest son of Dhṛitarāṣhṭra, rival of the Pāṇḍavas and chief antagonist in the *Mahabhārata* epic, often cited as an example of the harmful effects of unrestrained ambition, jealousy, and pride.

Dvārakā: ancient capital of Kṛiṣhṇa's kingdom now in Western Gujarat.

dvēṣha: aversion.

Ēkādaśhī: eleventh day of the lunar fortnight on which fasting is traditionally observed.

gaṇas: class of celestial beings, associated with looking after cosmic functions.

Gaṇēśha: deity with an elephant head and human body, son of Lord Śhiva and Goddess Pārvatī, and leader of the *gaṇas*.

Gaṅgā (Ganga): mighty and most sacred river in India. Known as the Ganges river in English.

gōpī: milkmaid from Vṛindāvan. The *gōpīs* were known for their ardent devotion to Lord Kṛiṣhṇa. Their devotion exemplifies the most intense love for God.

gṛihastha: householder; member of the second of four *āśhramas* (stages of life).

guṇa: quality in general; one of three types of qualities, viz. *sattva*, *rajas* and *tamas*. Human beings express a combination of these qualities. *Sattvic* qualities are associated with calmness and wisdom, *rajasic* with activity and restlessness, and *tamasic* with dullness or apathy.

guṇātīta: freed from or beyond all properties, especially the three *guṇas* (modes or qualities of nature).

guru: spiritual teacher.

gurukula: traditional school where children live with a guru who instructs them in scriptural and academic knowledge, while instilling spiritual values.

Hanumān: the *vānara* (monkey) disciple and companion of Rāma and one of the key characters in the *Rāmāyaṇa.*

haṭha yōga: physical exercises or *āsanas* designed to enhance one's overall well-being by toning the body and opening the various subtle channels of the body to promote the free flow of energy; the science of *prāṇāyama* (breath control), which includes other aspects of *yōga*, including *āsanas* and *mudrās* (esoteric hand gestures that express specific energies or powers).

Hiraṇyakaśhipu: powerful demon king and father of Prahlāda who was slain by Narasiṁha, the man-lion incarnation of Lord Viṣhṇu.

hōma: ancient Vedic fire ritual in which oblations are offered to the gods by offering ghee into a consecrated fire.

Indra: King of the Dēvas. He is associated with the sky, lightning, weather, thunder, storms, rains, river flows, and war.

irumuḍikkeṭṭu: a cloth bundle carried by pilgrims on their journey to Sabarimala, a famous temple in Kerala dedicated to Lord Ayyappa. The term '*irumuḍi*' literally means 'two bundles,' as the bundle is actually divided into two compartments within a cloth bundle. One side contains the sacred offering for the deity, such as ghee-filled coconuts, while the other holds provisions for the pilgrim's personal use during the journey. The *irumuḍikkeṭṭu* is placed on the pilgrim's head as a symbol of devotion and is offered to the deity upon reaching the temple.

iṣhṭa-dēvatā: preferred form of divinity.

īśhvara: God.

Itihāsas: the two great epics *Rāmāyaṇa* and *Mahābhārata*.

japa: repeated chanting of a *mantra*.

jīva: individual self or soul.

jīvanmukta: one who is spiritually liberated while alive.

jñāna: knowledge of the truth. A *jñānī* is one who knows the truth.

jñāna yōga: the path of knowledge.

jñānēndriyas : organs of knowledge/perception.

jñānī: a person who has realized God or the self; one who knows the truth.

Kālī: Goddess of fearsome aspect; depicted as dark, wearing a garland of skulls, and a girdle of human arms; feminine of *kāla* (time).

Kali Yuga: the present dark age of materialism and ignorance (see *yuga*).

Kālīdāsa: great devotee of Mother Kālī who was a renowned classical Sanskrit poet and playwright.

kāma: lust, or desire in general.

Kāmadēva: god of romantic and sensual desire.

karma: action; mental, verbal, and physical activity; chain of effects produced by our actions.

karma kāṇḍa: ritualistic portion of the *Vēdas.*

karma-phala: results of previous actions.

karma yōga: the way of action, the path of selfless service.

Kāśhī (Kashi): another name for the holy city of Varanasi in Uttar Pradesh.

Kauravas: the one hundred children of King Dhṛitarāṣhṭra and Queen Gāndhārī, of whom the unrighteous Duryōdhana was the eldest. The Kauravas were the enemies of their cousins, the virtuous Pāṇḍavas, whom they fought against in the *Mahābhārata* war.

Kayādhu: Hiraṇyakaśhipu's wife, mother of Prahlāda.

Kṛiṣhṇa: from *'kṛiṣh,'* meaning 'to draw to oneself' or 'to remove sin;' principal incarnation of Lord Viṣhṇu. He was born into a royal family but raised by foster parents, and lived as a cowherd boy in Vṛindāvan, where he was loved and worshiped by his devoted companions, the *gōpīs* (milkmaids) and *gōpas* (cowherd boys). Kṛiṣhṇa later established the city of Dvārakā. He was a friend and advisor to his cousins, the Pāṇḍavas, especially Arjuna, whom he served as charioteer during the *Mahābhārata* war, and to whom he revealed his teachings as the *Bhagavad Gītā*.

Kṛiṣhṇa Bhāva: 'the divine mood of Kṛiṣhṇa,' occasions when Amma revealed her oneness with Lord Kṛiṣhṇa.

kriyā yōga: 'yōga of action' defined in the *Patañjali Yōga Sūtras* to consist of three main practices: *tapaḥ* (austerity or self-discipline), *svādhyāya* (self-study or study of scriptures), and īśhvara *praṇidhāna* (devotion or surrender to God). It could also be interpreted more generally as a set of yōgic techniques for purifying the mind, controlling the sense organs and body, and attaining spiritual awakening.

kuṇḍalinī: 'the serpent power.' The spiritual energy, which rests like a coiled snake at the base of the spine. Through spiritual practices it is made to rise through the *suṣhumṇā* canal, a subtle nerve within the spine, and move up through the *chakras* (power centers). As the *kuṇḍalinī* rises from *chakra* to *chakra*, the spiritual aspirant begins to experience finer, more subtle levels of consciousness. The *kuṇḍalinī* finally reaches the highest *chakra* at the top of the head, the *sahasrāra*. This process of the awakening of *kuṇḍalinī* leads to self-realization.

Laṅka: name of Rāvaṇa's kingdom popularly believed to have been located in present day Sri Lanka.

liṅga: 'symbol,' 'defining sign.' A *śhivaliṅga* is typically an elongated oval stone or other material worshiped as embodiment of Lord Śhiva.

lōkāḥ samastāḥ sukhinō bhavantu: 'May all beings in all the worlds be happy.' A prayer for universal peace and wellbeing.

Mahābhārata: ancient Indian epic that Sage Vyāsa composed, depicting the war between the righteous Pāṇḍavas and the unrighteous Kauravas.

mahātmā: 'great soul;' term used to describe one who has attained spiritual realization.

mānasa-puṣhpa: metaphorical heart-flower or flower of the mind.

mañchāḍi: *Adenanthera pavonina* is a perennial leguminous tree very common in Kerala. Its seeds are known as 'mañchāḍi kuru' or 'red lucky seeds' and are like pebbles of bright red color.

mantra: a sound, syllable, word or words of spiritual content and power. According to

Vedic commentators, *mantras* are revelations of *ṛiṣhis* arising from deep contemplation.

Mārkaṇḍēya: revered sage known for his profound devotion to Lord Śhiva. Although destined to die at a young age, the boy received the boon of eternal life through his rigorous austerities.

mauna: vow/austerity of keeping silence.

mithyā: changing, therefore impermanent; also, illusory or untrue. According to *Advaita Vēdānta*, the entire visible world is *mithyā*.

mōkṣha: spiritual liberation, i.e. release from the cycle of births and deaths.

muhūrta: auspicious time.

naivēdyam: offering of eatables to a deity or idol, which may afterwards be distributed as *prasād* (blessed offering).

nāmajapa: continuous repetition of divine names.

Nārada: wandering sage ever engaged in singing the praises of Viṣhṇu. He composed the *Nārada Bhakti Sūtras*, aphorisms on devotion.

Narakāsura: demon king known for his tyranny and evil deeds, most famous for kidnapping thousands of women. He was eventually slain by Lord Kṛiṣhṇa, who also freed the women.

Narasiṁha: the fourth *avatār* (incarnation) of Lord Viṣhṇu in the form of a man-lion, who saved the devoted boy Prahlāda from his wicked father, the demon king Hiraṇyakaśhipu.

Nārāyaṇa: another name of Viṣhṇu.

Navarātri: 'nine nights' of worship of the three aspects of the Divine Mother, as Durgā, Lakṣhmī, and Sarasvatī.

nirākāra: devoid of form (opposite of *sakāra*).

nirguṇa: without attributes (opposite of *saguṇa*).

niśhkriyā: actionless or inactive; characterized by a state of inaction (opposite of *sakriyā*).

niṣhṭha: dedication, devotion; excellence.

nitya-anitya vivēka: an advaitic methodology of discerning between the eternal and the transient.

niyama: positive duties or observances (the 'dos'); the second 'limb' of the *aṣhṭāṅga yōga* (eight limbs) formulated by Sage Patañjali, and they include *śhaucha* (purity), *santōṣha* (contentment), *tapas* (austerity), *svādhyāya* (scriptural study) and *īśhvara-praṇidhāna* (contemplation of God); often mentioned in association with *yama*.

pāda pūjā: ceremonial washing of the feet as a form of worship.

pañcha mahā yajñas: five great sacrifices to be performed daily by householders, viz. *brahma-yajña* (studying/teaching the *Vēdas*); the *tarpaṇa* (offering libations of water to deceased ancestors) is *pitṛu-yajña*; the *hōma* is *dēva-yajña* (offerings to the gods); the *bali* (offering a portion of the daily meal of rice, grain, ghee, etc., to all creatures) is *bhūta-yajña*; and the honoring of guests is *nṛu-yajña* or *manuṣhya-yajña*.

Pāñchālī: another name for Draupadī, the wife of the five Pāṇḍava brothers.

Pāṇḍavas: five sons of King Pāṇḍu, and cousins of Kṛiṣhṇa, who are the main protagonists in the great *Mahābhārata* epic.

paramēśhvara: supreme lord.

paramparā: transmission of knowledge and practices within a lineage or tradition.

Pārvatī: consort of Lord Śhiva.

payasam: sweet pudding.

phala-śhruti: description of the results obtained from recitation of a chant.

prakṛiti: nature; primal matter.

pramāṇa: source or means of knowledge.

prāṇa: vital force.

praṇava: the mystic syllable 'Ōm'.

prārabdha: also known as *prārabdha karma*, the results of past actions that are the cause of one's birth and whose effects one is destined to experience in this lifetime.

prasād: blessed offering or gift from a holy person or temple, often in the form of food.

prēma: deep love.

prēma-bhakti: highest form of love for God.

pūjā: ritualistic or ceremonial worship.

pūjārī: one who performs ritualistic or ceremonial worship. *Pūjāriṇī* is the female equivalent.

pundit: scholar; knowledgeable person.

Purāṇas: compendium of stories, including the biographies and stories of gods, saints, kings, and great people; allegories and chronicles of great historical events that aim to make the teachings of the *Vēdas* simple and available to all.

Puranic: pertaining to the *Purāṇas.*

puruṣha: the unmoving, eternal consciousness (according to *Sāṅkhya* philosophy) that witnesses the dynamic unfolding of *prakṛiti* (primordial nature); 'man' or 'human being'; it can also represent the supreme, universal being.

puruṣhārtha: the four goals of human life, namely *dharma* (righteous living), *artha* (pursuit of wealth), *kāma* (desire fulfillment), and *mōkṣha* (liberation from delusion).

puṣhpaka-vimāna: flying chariot of Rāvaṇa, later used by Rāma to return with Sītā to Ayōdhyā.

puṣhpāñjali: offering of flowers.

rāga: attachment; passion.

rājā yōga: literally 'royal path' to spiritual enlightenment emphasizing meditation and mind control. It is often associated with the eight-limbs (*aṣhṭāṅga*) of Sage Patañjali laid out in the *Yōga Sūtras.*

rajas: activity; passion. One of the three guṇas or fundamental qualities of nature (see *guṇa*).

rajōguṇa: activity; passion. One of the three *guṇas* or fundamental qualities of nature.

rākṣhasa: demonic beings that derive pleasure from tormenting others.

Rāma: 'the giver of joy.' The divine hero of the *Rāmāyaṇa*. An incarnation of Lord Viṣhṇu, he is considered the ideal man of *dharma* and virtue.

Rāmāyaṇa: 24,000-verse epic poem on the life and times of Lord Rāma.

rāsa-līlā: mystic dance in which Lord Kṛiṣhṇa danced with the *gōpīs* (milkmaids) of Vṛindāvan. He manifested as many identical forms of himself as there were gōpīs, thus leading each one of them to think that the Lord was dancing with her alone.

Ratnākara: name of the highway robber who transformed into the great sage Vālmīki by chanting the name of Lord Rāma with the blessings of the Seven Sages.

Rāvaṇa: powerful demon. Viṣhṇu incarnated as Lord Rāma to kill him and thereby restore harmony to the world.

ṛiṣhi: seer to whom *mantras* are revealed in deep meditation. Also the authors of many scriptural texts.

sāgara: ocean.

saguṇa: with attributes (opposite of *nirguṇa*).

sakāra: with form (opposite of *nirākāra*).

sakriyā: active or engaged in actions; characterized by the performance of actions (opposite of *niśhkriyā*).

samarpaṇam: handing completely over, surrendering.

samaṣhṭi: the collective; aggregate of all parts.

sampradāya: spiritual tradition or school that has its own distinct doctrines, practices, and beliefs, often passed down through a lineage of teachers and disciples.

saṁsāra: the cycle of birth and death; the world of plurality.

saṁskāra: imprints or impressions left on the mind as a result of past experiences, actions, and thoughts (in this birth and also in prior births). These imprints shape an individual's character, tendencies, and reactions in future situations. *Saṁskāra* can also refer to the prevailing culture, or a particular deep-seated conditioning that shapes individuals, families, and society. The ritualistic ceremonies performed at significant stages of life, such as birth, marriage, and death, are also called *saṁskāras*.

sanātana: eternal.

Sanātana Dharma: 'Eternal Way of Life,' the original and traditional name of Hinduism.

sannyāsa: a formal vow of renunciation.

sannyāsī: a person who has renounced the material world, including family, career, and other attachments, to pursue a life devoted to spiritual practice and the pursuit of enlightenment or liberation (*mōkṣha*).

Sanskrit: language of the oldest sacred text, the *Ṛig Vēda*, and the other three *Vēdas*; the language of most ancient Hindu scriptures.

Sarasvatī: goddess of learning and the arts. Also the name of a sacred river.

sarvaṁ brahmamayaṁ: 'all is pervaded by brahman.'

sattva: goodness, purity, serenity. One of the three guṇas or fundamental qualities of nature (see *guṇa*).

sēvā: selfless service, the results of which are dedicated to God.

sēvaka (sēvak): servant.

śhakti: power; energy.

Śhakti: the personification of cosmic will and energy, representing the dynamic counterpart to Śhiva (the unmoving principle).

Ṣhaṣhṭhī: sixth day of the lunar fortnight on which a particular form of Dēvī is worshiped.

Śhiva: the static aspect of *brahman* as the male principle. Worshiped as the first in the lineage of gurus, and as the formless substratum of the universe in relation to the creative principle, Śhakti. He is the Lord of Destruction in the trinity of Brahmā (Lord of Creation), Viṣhṇu (Lord of Preservation), and Śhiva. Usually depicted as a monk, with his body covered in ash, snakes in his hair and adorning his neck and arms, wearing only a loincloth; he carries a begging bowl and a trident in his hands.

śhivaliṅga: a symbol of Lord Śhiva representing the formless, infinite nature of the divine.

Śhivarātri: annual festival also known as *Mahā Śhivarātri*, 'the great night of Lord Shiva.'

śhraddhā: attentiveness; faith.

Śhrīhari: another name of Viṣhṇu.

smṛiti: 'what is remembered;' refers to sacred Hindu texts that are attributed to *ṛiṣhis.*

śhrī (sri): a title of respect originally meaning 'divine,' 'holy,' or 'auspicious.'

svara yōga: the path of using breathing exercises to attain self-realization.

svarūpa: one's own form or true nature.

tāli: traditional wedding pendant. This is the Malayalam equivalent of the *maṅgalasūtra* in Sanskrit.

tamas: darkness; inertia; apathy; ignorance. *Tamas* is one of the three *guṇas* or fundamental qualities of nature.

tamasic: of the nature of *tamas.*

tamōguṇa: darkness; inertia; apathy; ignorance. One of the three *guṇas* or fundamental qualities of nature.

tantra: an extensive tradition encompassing ritualistic practices, worship of deities, and traditional texts often featuring dialogues between Śhiva and Śhakti. It includes methods for developing the hidden, latent power in individuals, leading to spiritual realization. Key practices involve worship of images (*archā*), diagrams (*yantra*), mystic syllables (*mantra*), and meditation (*upāsana*). In general, all practices aimed at raising consciousness from the limited self to universal consciousness are considered part of *tantra*. These practices may also be used to fulfill worldly desires.

tapas (tapasya): austerities, penance.

tapasvī: one engaged in *tapas* or spiritual austerities.

tattva: essence; substratum; spiritual principle; underlying truth.

tyāga: giving up, renunciation.

upādhi: limiting adjunct, e.g. name, form, attribute; instrument; tool. A means that conditions something else by transferring its properties to that other thing on account of the proximity between them. The standard illustration is that of a red flower which transfers its property of redness to a clear crystal due to their proximity. In this case the red flower is the *upādhi* of the crystal.

upavāsa: vow/austerity of fasting.

vairāgī: a person who has cultivated a deep sense of detachment from worldly pleasures and material possessions.

vairāgya: dispassion.

Vālmīki: sage and author of the *Rāmāyaṇa.*

vānaprastha: 'forest life;' a reference to the retired life dedicated to spiritual practices; the third of the four stages of life (see *āśhrama*).

vāsanā: latent tendency or subtle desire that manifests as thought, motive and action; subconscious impression gained from experience.

vasudhaiva kuṭumbakam: 'the world as one family' — a popular phrase from *Mahā Upaniṣhad*, 6.72.

Vēdas: the most ancient of all scriptures. Originating from God, the *Vēdas* were not composed by any human author but were 'revealed' in deep meditation to the ancient seers. These revelations came to be known as the *Vēdas*, of which there are four: *Ṛig*, *Yajur*, *Sāma*, and *Atharva.*

Vibhīṣhaṇa: younger demon-brother of Rāvaṇa who speaks out against the unrighteousness of his brother and subsequently surrenders himself to Lord Rāma.

vigraha: lit. 'shape; form; figure.' Physical representation or manifestation of a deity, such as a statue or an image used for worship.

viṣhavaidya: traditional healer specializing in treating snakebite and other venomous conditions.

Viṣhṇu: 'all-pervader,' Lord of Sustenance in the trinity of Brahmā (Lord of Creation), Viṣhṇu, and Śhiva (Lord of Destruction).

viśhvāsa: faith.

vivēka-buddhi: the aspect of intellect involved in discerning and distinguishing between what is true and false, right and wrong; it enables clarity of judgment and wisdom in decision-making.

vrata: religious vow or observance.

vyaṣhṭi: individual; a part of the whole.

yajña: sacred acts of worship performed with the intent of offering something to the divine. Traditionally, a *yajña* consists of oblations offered into a sacred fire according to scriptural injunctions accompanied by the chanting of sacred *mantras*. In a broader sense, a *yajña* can also comprise an act of selflessness performed with the intention of offering something for the welfare of others.

yama: restraints for proper conduct (the 'don'ts'); the first 'limb' of the *aṣhṭānga yōga* (eight limb path) formulated by Sage Patañjali. They include *ahiṁsā* (non-violence), *satya* (truthfulness), *astēya* (non-stealing), *brahmacharya* (chastity) and *aparigraha* (non-covetousness); often mentioned in association with *niyama*.

yōga: 'to unite.' Union with the supreme being. A broad term, it also refers to the various methods of practices through which one can attain oneness with the divine. A path that leads to self-realization.

Yōga Sūtras: '*Patañjali Yōga Sūtras*,' aphorisms composed by Sage Patañjali on the path to purification and transcendence of the mind.

yōgī: a practitioner or an adept of *yōga*; *yoginī* is the female equivalent.

yuga: according to the Hindu worldview, the universe (from origin to dissolution) passes through a cycle made up of four *yugas* or ages. The first is *Kṛita* or *Satya Yuga*, during which *dharma* reigns in society. Each succeeding age sees the progressive decline of *dharma*. The second age is known as *Trēta Yuga*, the third is *Dvāpara Yuga*, and the fourth and present epoch is known as *Kali Yuga*.

Index of Questions

1. What is the difference between the Hindu religion and other religions? 23

2. Who is the founder of the Hindu religion? 27

3. Is Sanātana Dharma the same as the Hindu religion? 29

4. Aren't the different paths in Hinduism a drawback? 32

5. Why does the Hindu religion have many paths? 33

6. What is the unique feature of the Hindu religion? 36

7. What is the difference between brahman and īśhvara? 40

8. What are the four goals of human life? 40

9. What is dharma? 41

10. What is mōkṣha? 45

11. The Hindu religion worships many Gods. In reality, is there more than one God? 47

12. In the Hindu religion, it is not unusual for human beings to be worshiped as God. We do not see this to such an extent in other religions. Why is it so? 53

13. In Sanātana Dharma, why is it said that the creator and creation are one? 55

14. If creation and creator are one, why do we not see God's omnipotence and omniscience in cats, dogs, and other life forms? 57

15. Kālī is portrayed as naked, wearing a garland of skulls, with weapons in her hands, and drinking blood. What is the meaning of worshiping such a Kālī? 59

16. Some people say that Gaṇēśha with his elephant head and human body is an illogical myth. What is Amma's response to this? 62

17. Some people consider the śhivaliṅga as indecent. Is there any foundation for this? 66

18. Śhiva is depicted wearing serpents as ornaments. What does this symbolize? 73

19. What does it mean when it's said that Śhiva lives in the cremation grounds? 74

20. What is māyā? How can we overcome it? 76

21. Does the Hindu religion reject materialism? 80

22. Does Amma recognize the various traditions and rituals of the Hindu religion? 82

23. Do we need to believe in God to become a Hindu? 83

24. Where is the need for faith in God in human life? 84

25. Is there anyone unfit or ineligible to follow the Hindu religion? 86

26. What is meant by surrendering or offering to God? 87

27. Ghee, honey, and other substances are sacrificed into the fire during a hōma to please God. Is it correct to waste them? It is said that many other objects of value are also sacrificed in the fire. What is Amma's opinion on this? 90

28. If God is everywhere, then why do we need temples? 95

29. Through temple worship, aren't we limiting the omnipresent God to a single idol? 99

30. What is the need for making oblations in temples? 102

31. The idols in temples are adorned with costly ornaments. Aren't such expensive adornments against devotion and spirituality? 110

32. What is the principle behind idol worship? 114

33. Is it possible to say when idol worship began? 117

34. Some people condemn the Hindu religion because of idol worship. Is there any truth to this? 125

35. Shouldn't we worship the sculptor more than the idol he sculpted? 127

36. Do those who go to temples understand the fundamental principles behind temple worship? 128

37. What is genuine devotion? 131

38. Amma, you say that we should have śhraddhā, bhakti, and viśhvāsa. What is meant by these? 136

39. It is said that devotion should be selfless. If so, is it wrong to pray to God to remove our sorrows? 138

40. How long do we have to pray every day to gain the experience of God? 140

41. Some people criticize devotion, faith in God, and spirituality, as superstitions and weaknesses of the mind that are used as instruments for exploitation. Can we say that such labeling is unfounded? 142

42. Some people cry and pray. Isn't this a weakness? Doesn't energy get dissipated through this? 149

43. Isn't it a sign of weakness to pray out loud? 151

44. Are there any benefits arising from singing devotional songs, praying, and chanting the Lord's names? 157

45. Are there any particular rules we need to observe to perform spiritual practices? 164

46. What is the importance of spiritual vows? 166

47. What is the benefit of pilgrimages? 172

48. Kṛiṣhṇa says in the Bhagavad Gītā that we only have the right to do actions but not to their fruit. Doesn't this mean that we should work but not ask for our wages? 178

49. What is the role of action and the fruit of action in our life? 182

50. Are the traditions of Hinduism logical? 185

51. How did wrong practices come into being? 186

52. Some people say that astrology is a superstitious belief. Is astrology helpful in facing life's problems? 188

53. What is the role of ātmā-kṛipā, the grace of one's own self, in our life? 190

54. Does the Hindu religion have the concept of everlasting hell? 193

55. Some people say that women should not chant the Lalitā Sahasranāma. It is also said that we incur sin if we make any mistakes in pronunciation while chanting. Is there any basis for these claims? 195

56. In this world, some are healthy, and some are sick. Some are rich, while others are poor.

Some are beautiful, while others are ugly. Is God partial? 197

57. The story of Kṛiṣhṇa stealing the clothes of the gōpīs and performing the rāsa-līlā with them is portrayed as 'indecent' by some people. 199

58. It is said that Śhrī Kṛiṣhṇa had sixteen thousand and eight wives. How can this be explained? 201

59. Why are birds and animals worshiped in the Hindu religion? 202

60. Aren't many of the Hindu religion's traditions primitive, including the worship of birds and animals? 204

61. Many people criticize the Hindu religion for its practice of animal sacrifice. Isn't what they say true? 207

62. Why is a monkey worshiped as God in the Hindu religion? 211

63. What are the pañcha mahā yajñas? 216

64. What is the need for spiritual texts? 220

65. Is mastery of Sanskrit needed to live a spiritual life? 225

66. What is the importance of the *Bhagavad Gītā*? 229

67. The *Purāṇas* contain many stories and allusions that are illogical. What is their significance? 231

68. The scriptures tell us that God is within us and not separate from us. If this is so, what is the need for a guru? 234

69. Isn't spirituality and sannyāsa a desertion from life's responsibilities? 236

70. Is knowledge of spirituality necessary to serve people? 239

71. Why has nature lost its rhythm to such a great extent? What solution does our culture have for nature's loss of rhythm and harmony? 246

72. What is the attitude of the Hindu religion towards those who follow other religions? 254

73. Don't some people allege that the dēvatās (deities) of the Hindu religion are demons? 256

74. What are Amma's views on religious conversion? 259

Pronunciation Guide

Vowels can be short or long:

a – as 'u' in 'but' **ā** – as 'a' in 'far'

e – as 'a' in 'may' **ē** – as 'a' in 'name'

i – as 'i' in 'pin' **ī** – as 'ee' in 'meet'

o – as in 'oh' **ō** – as 'o' in 'mole'

u – as 'u' in 'push' **ū** – as 'oo' in 'hoot'

ṛi – as 'ri' in 'rim' **ṛu** – as 'ru' in Spanish 'Peru'

ḥ – pronounce: **aḥ** like 'aha,' **iḥ** like 'ihi,' **uḥ** like 'uhu,' **ēḥ** like 'ēhē,' and **ōḥ** like 'ōhō.'

Some consonants are aspirated (e.g. kh); others are not (e.g. k):

k – as 'k' in 'kite' **kh** – as 'ckh' in 'Eckhart'

g – as 'g' in 'give' **gh** – as 'g-h' in 'dig-hard'

ch – as 'ch' in 'chat' **chh** – as 'ch-h' in 'staunch-heart'

j – as 'j' in 'joy' **jh** – as 'dgeh' in 'hedgehog'

p – as 'p' in 'pine' **ph** – as 'ph' in 'up-hill'

b – as 'b' in 'bird' **bh** – as 'bh' in 'rub-hard'

Pronounced with the tip of the tongue against the teeth:

t – as 't' in 'teach' **th** – as 'th' in 'anthill'

d – as 'd' in 'door' **dh** – as 'dh' in 'madhouse'

n – as 'n' in 'night'

Retroflex sounds are produced by rolling the tongue back with the tip touching the roof of the mouth. The following examples can be used for practice:

ṭ – as 't' in 'tub' **ṭh** – as 'th' in 'lighthouse'

ḍ – as 'd' in 'dove' **ḍh** – as 'dh' in 'red-hot'

ṇ – as 'n' in 'naught'

ḷ – as 'l' in 'revelry' **ṣh** – as 'sh' in 'shine'

zh – 'rr' in 'hurray' *(in Malayalam and Tamil)*

Other consonants:

y – as 'y' in 'yes' **r** – as 'R' in Italian 'Roma'

l – as 'l' in 'like' **v** – as 'v' in 'void'

śh – as 'sh' in 'shepherd' **s** – as 's' in 'sun'

m – as 'm' in 'mother' **h** – as 'h' in 'hot'

ṅ – as 'ng' in 'sing' **ñ** – as 'ny' in 'canyon'

Double consonants:

chch – as 'tc' in 'hot chip'

jj – as 'dj' in 'red jet'

www.ingramcontent.com/pod-product-compliance
Lightning Source LLC
Chambersburg PA
CBHW070137100426
42743CB00013B/2738
* 9 7 8 1 6 8 0 3 7 8 6 1 0 *